DESIGNING AN
ANTHROPOLOGY CAREER

DESIGNING AN ANTHROPOLOGY CAREER

Professional Development Exercises

Sherylyn H. Briller
and Amy Goldmacher

ALTAMIRA
PRESS

A Division of Rowman & Littlefield Publishers, Inc.
Lanham • New York • Toronto • Plymouth, UK

A Note on the Cover Image: The cover photo was taken by James Hanggi in Amboseli, Kenya. We chose it as the cover art because we liked the metaphor of the open road and how the career possibilities for anthropologists can be seen as wide open. Please note that even though the road is going somewhere in one direction, various people have made different choices about how to approach this open road, as evidenced by the different tracks you see in the picture. Similarly, we hope that you will use this book to help you journey in your way along the road in designing your own anthropological career!

ALTAMIRA PRESS
A division of Rowman & Littlefield Publishers, Inc.
A wholly owned subsidiary of The Rowman & Littlefield Publishing Group, Inc.
4501 Forbes Boulevard, Suite 200
Lanham, MD 20706
www.altamirapress.com

Estover Road
Plymouth PL6 7PY
United Kingdom

British Library Cataloguing in Publication Information Available

Library of Congress Cataloguing-in-Publication Data

Briller, Sherylyn H., 1968–
  Designing an anthropology career : professional development exercises / Sherylyn H. Briller and Amy Goldmacher.
    p. cm.
  ISBN-13: 978-0-7591-0942-1 (cloth : alk. paper)
  ISBN-10: 0-7591-0942-7 (cloth : alk. paper)
  ISBN-13: 978-0-7591-0943-8 (pbk. : alk. paper)
  ISBN-10: 0-7591-0943-5 (pbk. : alk. paper)
  eISBN-13: 978-0-7591-1305-3
  eISBN-10: 0-7591-1305-X
 1. Anthropology—Vocational guidance. I. Goldmacher, Amy, 1973– II. Title.

  GN41.8.B75 2009
  301.023—dc22   2008029163

Printed in the United States of America

♾™ The paper used in this publication meets the minimum requirements of American National Standard for Information Sciences—Permanence of Paper for Printed Library Materials, ANSI/NISO Z39.48–1992.

Contents

Acknowledgments

The authors acknowledge the anthropology students at Wayne State University who enthusiastically did these exercises, brought new insights every time they were used, and continually motivated the authors with their experiences. Special thanks to the following students who gave permission for their sample exercises to be printed in the book: Elena Barbulescu, Mary Durocher, Amy Goldmacher, Andrea Grady, Angela Guy-Lee, Dianna Jakubiec, Anne Katz, Jasmine Ligenza-Posante, Terri Ann Liller, Marlo Jenkins, Lindsey Martin, Elizabeth Nanas, Monica Rodriguez, and Jennifer VanNuil.

We also acknowledge our families, friends, and colleagues who heard about, gave feedback, and provided support as the project developed over time. Sherylyn Briller specifically thanks James and Michael Hanggi for understanding all of the time that she needed to spend writing this book.

I

DESIGNING AN ANTHROPOLOGY CAREER

1

Introduction

Congratulations, you've picked one of the most exciting fields to study. Learning about human variation and diversity over time and in different places is fascinating. You will most likely find your anthropology courses filled with other adventurous, curious, broad-minded people like yourself. Many people studying anthropology describe discovering this field as a homecoming of sorts. In this realm, eclectic backgrounds and perspectives and strong skills as generalists are appreciated and valued rather than simply considered odd. Whereas you may have tried a number of other fields and considered yourself an academic black sheep, you suddenly find yourself surrounded by like-minded people. This discovery can be a great experience, and you may heartily enjoy your anthropological education and those you interact with in school and in the field. Oftentimes you hear those new to anthropology say in wonderment, "I didn't know that something like this field was out there."

Although you may be thrilled with the subject matter, studying anthropology is still a path less trodden. Others may not readily understand your passion for this subject and consider it esoteric, not useful, not employable, or all of the above. Consequently, they may criticize your choice of field of study as impractical and irresponsible—and in extreme cases, they may feel that you have lost your mind entirely. At this point they may try to intervene by talking about a bad economy, scary job market, and limited career options. Indeed, family and community pressures may be intense to persuade you to do something else that is more lucrative, less risky, something that other people will have heard of and may more easily understand. In the face of such adversity, an anthropology advisor has remarked that she thinks it takes real courage for some people to defy family and community expectations of more traditional or well-known careers and to continue their study of anthropology.

Anthropology is a discipline that draws students while they are in school, and also attracts people who are considering changing jobs or adding new dimensions to their careers. Many people are attracted to anthropology because they develop a passion for the subject matter when they are exposed to it as part of their liberal arts education. Others come across situations in their work lives where they intuitively know anthropology would be useful, but may not know how to articulate its value to others. A common concern for those studying anthropology is how to link it to career goals. Many jobs outside of the discipline of anthropology call for anthropological skills. For example, a search on Monster.com using the keyword "anthropology" results in job listings in areas of publishing, software support, product design, health research, government, and law enforcement. You can see that there are many occasions to use anthropological skills in a variety of fields, so a background in anthropology can broaden your job prospects!

Although the magic of anthropology attracts students to the field, the challenge of navigating a nonlinear career path can seem quite daunting. Fields like medicine and law have more obvious career paths: one goes to medical school to become a doctor and to law school to become a lawyer. The relationship between an anthropology education and an anthropological career path is often less clear than those mentioned above. Thus, in anthropology classes, there are often conversations in which traditional undergraduates worry about rocky starts to their careers and nontraditional students worry about bumpy career transitions. These fears about risk, uncertainty, and short- and long-term employment prospects often result in conversations like those given in Table I.1.1. Our aim is to enable you to have these conversations and address the career concerns raised by others and that you may have as well.

The idea for developing this book came about because Wayne State University anthropology students of all ages and with diverse life experi-

Table I.1.1. The Conversation

Traditional Undergraduate Students May Say	Nontraditional Students May Say
I *love* anthropology but I'm worried about . . . . . . getting a job . . . making a living . . . paying my rent . . . being continuously employed . . . being able to move out of my parents' house	I *love* anthropology but I'm worried about . . . . . . getting a well-paying job . . . making an adequate living . . . paying my mortgage . . . being able to retire . . . being able to put shoes on my children's feet

ences frequently said that the curriculum did not allow enough space for them to explore working in anthropology as well as studying anthropology. A good workbook titled *Careers in Anthropology*, first published about ten years ago, offered students ways to explore their personal fit with working in this field and gave practical suggestions to help them start their careers (Omohundro 2001). However, two limitations exist with using this career resource: its content is mainly geared at traditional undergraduate students in bachelor of arts programs in anthropology, and the book has unfortunately now gone out of print!

We found that our Wayne State students were similarly asking for more knowledge of how to explain an anthropological background and skills and justify why their backgrounds and skills were relevant to the jobs for which they were applying. However, our student population, which includes many nontraditional students, wanted to know much more about how to successfully incorporate their extensive life and work experiences into successfully finding anthropologically oriented employment. For many nontraditional students, they implicitly recognized that they would be taking their anthropology skill set into other job realms, but they wanted to learn more about how to effectively do so. In a university well known for its applied specializations, including medical and business anthropology, hearing this message was sobering. As we went to professional conferences and spoke to those from other institutions, we realized that we were already doing more than many anthropology departments in this area. Yet our students had told us loud and clear that the current level of professional preparation was not adequate and did not fully address how they should deal with the complexities of their individual situations.

We hope that this book and its customized exercises will help up-and-coming anthropologists and those further along in their careers to master the anthropological "tools in their own professional toolkit" (NAPA/AAA 2000) (see Table I.1.2). The toolkit was originally developed by the National Association for the Practice of Anthropology (NAPA) to formally describe and identify the perspectives, methods, skills, attributes, applications, and challenges that anthropology brings when applied to real-world problems (Garcia Ruiz 2000). From our experiences at Wayne State, we have seen that this toolkit is a useful teaching device to help students conceptualize what anthropologists do in their workplaces. Specifically, this tool is useful to help anthropology students and professionals reflect on their backgrounds, skill sets, and the complementarity of an anthropological approach for other fields. Importantly, this toolkit also gives students a sense of how to talk about their own abilities and educate potential employers as well as others about how anthropologists approach and solve problems and the contributions they can make.

Table I.1.2. The Toolkit of a Good Professional Anthropologist

PERSPECTIVE (Our Core Approach)	METHODS (What We Own/Use—italicized if we own it)	SKILLS (How We Do It)	ANTHROPOLOGICAL ATTRIBUTES (Informs Use of Methods)	PROFESSIONAL ATTRIBUTES (Needed to Be Effective)	EXAMPLES OF APPLICATIONS (What We Do)	CHALLENGES (To Enhance Our Professionalism)
Holistic	*Ethnography*	Finding themes and patterns	Ability to work in teams as collaborators	Ability to work in teams as collaborators	Time-limited, focused, product-oriented work	Engagement and disengagement
Systemic	*Interactive, systematic participation in observing*	Cultural brokering	Adaptability	Can-do orientation	Advocacy research	Social skills
Integrative	Structured, systematic observation	Translating	Advocacy orientation	Entrepreneurial	Analyst	Good work habits
Contextual	Analysis	Teaching	Approachability	Multidisciplinary orientation	Administration	Public relations
Comparative	Focus groups	Interpreting and presenting others' views	Multiple lenses	Understanding of qualitative methods	Policy making	Positive professional presentation of selves
Cross-cultural	Rapid assessments	Speaking and writing clearly	Flexibility	Business skills	Planning	Borders with other disciplines
People-oriented	Interviewing	Building trust	Risk-taker	Technology skills	Training	Lines/boundaries of our work
Relativistic	Evaluation	Storytelling	Good work habits		Program services and research design	Fieldwork experience in all professional training

Emic and etic valuation	Testing analysis with informants	Narrating	Participatory		Service provision	Disseminating our methods and outcomes
Recognition of complexity	Qualitative and quantitative research	Facilitating	Listening skills		Therapy	Developing support networks
Focus on process	Iterative approach to research	Integrating disparate parts into a whole	Respectful		Product R&D	
Collaborative	Secondary and archival research	Systematizing/ using complex information	Learner		Program evaluation	
We ask what the questions are before we ask for answers	Research design	Inductive and deductive reasoning	Curious, inquisitive		Sales and marketing	
Theoretically informed	Data collection	Marketing ideas or projects	Nonjudgmental	Mediation	Teaching	
	Data management					

Reprinted with permission from *Anthropology News*, March 2000, 41(3):44.

We encourage you to make use of this toolkit as you do the exercises in this book. One aspect that we particularly like about this toolkit is how it presents categories of information in a grid format, and we have seen that anthropology students like that feature as well. Thinking about your anthropology career for the first time or revisiting your career later is inherently complex and requires organizing your wide-ranging thoughts. Like the Toolkit of a Good Professional Anthropologist, we designed our exercises to frequently include a grid or other worksheet-type format to use as you assemble your thoughts regarding a specific career-related topic. You can decide how to most usefully bring together the toolkit's formal categories and your own background and skill set. Some people may want to read an exercise's description and instructions and look at the toolkit before preparing their own responses. Alternatively, others may want to plunge right in and record their own ideas and reactions first and then compare their responses with the toolkit's categories. Whichever the case may be, combining these tools can be a powerful strategy for organizing your anthropological career documents and related materials.

Being confident about what your anthropological skill set is and knowing that you do not need to leave it behind, regardless of where your career path takes you, are both very important. Many times people tell us that they took an anthropology class in college (or even majored in the subject) and really loved it but that they never used anthropology again. This is a most unfortunate state of affairs for our field. Some good news is that there are increasing employment opportunities for anthropologists if you know how to look for and recognize them. More good news is that anthropological work is often fascinating, intellectually challenging, and the kind of thing you envisioned doing. Working with people, opportunities to travel, and diverse job duties all contribute to the discipline being characterized as out of the ordinary. Simply put, if you go to a party and tell people that you are an anthropologist, there will not be the same reaction as saying you are an accountant. Although anthropology is often inaccurately portrayed in movies such as the Indiana Jones series and the popular forensic anthropology-related television shows, the exciting and adventurous aspects of the field are brought to light. Thus, people rightly have the impression that anthropology is not the kind of career where you just show up, do repetitive work, punch a clock, and go home. As in any job, there are parts of the work that can be quite tedious, but there are other aspects that well compensate for it. Overall, most anthropologists will tell you that their jobs are very interesting with a good mix of job-related activities. After all, this is the kind of field that people contemplate shifting into when they are looking for something more, not vice versa. What needs to be put right in anthropological education today is helping students develop the mindset that they can continue to draw upon their anthropological background in diverse career realms and over time, and that the world would be a better place for them doing so!

In Textboxes I.1.1 and I.1.2 we offer our personal histories to show how we developed this mindset and how since receiving undergraduate degrees in anthropology, we have been working and providing for ourselves and our families consistently. Please note that we have each often worked under different titles than "anthropologist," but we have always used our field's approaches and skills and saw ourselves as working anthropologically.

Textbox I.1.1.   Autobiographical Account by Sherylyn H. Briller

I come from a family of urban teachers. My father taught for thirty years in the New York City public school system. Although he truly made a difference in his students' lives, this job was very demanding. As I was growing up, he often came home bone-weary and said, "You can pick any profession you like, just don't be a teacher. It's too exhausting." Today, I teach anthropology at Wayne State, a large urban university in Detroit. This career choice is doubly ironic because of my father's warning and I did not envision myself becoming a professor. On the first day of each course, I always tell students "my story," and I will share it with you now.

Like many students in these classes, I was a twenty-one-year-old undergraduate anthropology major who did not know what I wanted to do after I finished college. I thought that I wanted to work in a field related to aging. In my family there were many elders, including grandparents and great aunts and uncles. Some of these elders were childless, and my nuclear family served as the "children" and "grandchildren" in their lives. I relished spending time with these elders and hearing their stories. I was interested in the "Greatest Generation" and their World War II memories before the newscaster Tom Brokaw popularized the term. This strong interest in working with elders and oral history drove me in the direction of gerontology.

My first job after college was working in a nursing home as an activities assistant. This job was very anthropological as you were charged with learning about people, their interests, and trying to incorporate what you found into making institutional living more palatable. I would like to say that I was hired because of my kind personality and rapport with elders. The reality was that my boss thought that a college graduate could keep up with the enormous amount of paperwork that the job required. This job also introduced me to working on special care units and the "culture of dementia care."

After nearly two years, I went to work as the program coordinator for a large community senior center in an economically depressed neighborhood in Minneapolis. Most of the elders qualified for various social services. My job involved running an activity program that encouraged elders to come to the center where they ate hot lunch, socialized, and were linked to supportive services. Technically, I was supposed to have an MSW (master of social work) degree for this job, but this did not prevent me from being hired. When I began working in the senior center, I eventually planned to go back to graduate school and get an MSW degree. However, I shared an office with the program's social worker and got to see her job firsthand. In my opinion, there were strong pros and cons to her job. On the positive side, she got to work with elders one on one every day. On the negative side, she spent much time telling seniors about their eligibility for services. Frequently, the regulations were problematic and the process was frustrating for all. Watching these experiences kindled my interest in aging research and policy. I was given the

Textbox I.1.1. (*continued*)

advice that to work in a policy-related area, I needed to go to graduate school and get an advanced degree. Yet, no one said that the advanced degree had to be in a specific field, so I chose to stick with anthropology.

I entered the graduate program at Case Western Reserve University in Cleveland, Ohio, where faculty specialized in medical anthropology and the anthropology of aging. I became very interested in cross-cultural gerontology. My dissertation research focused on familial and governmental old age support mechanisms in Mongolia. I consider myself very lucky to have had this traditional long-term ethnographic fieldwork experience in Asia as a key part of my graduate education. While in graduate school, I also worked on an interdisciplinary research team focused on improving U.S. long-term care environments. We did research, staff education, and consulting and published a book series on creating successful dementia care settings.

As I was finishing my dissertation, I was offered a one-year position as a lecturer in the Department of Anthropology at Wayne State University. The next year I was offered a tenure track job as an assistant professor. My current research program focuses mainly on aging and end-of-life issues in the United States. With colleagues, I recently edited an interdisciplinary book examining end-of-life issues. I consider myself to be an applied anthropologist. While my home institution is a university, I am highly interested in using anthropology to address aging and health-related issues impacting multiple constituencies. Importantly, my job also involves training other anthropologists to effectively work in a broad range of community settings.

There are multiple purposes in my telling this story to my classes. First, it helps students get acquainted with me and learn about some of the experiences that have shaped my career development. Second, the story is meant to reassure them that it is fine to study anthropology because you are interested in the subject, even if you do not know precisely how you will use the knowledge in the future. Third, the story illustrates how the path into a field like medical anthropology is often not linear. Fourth, I explain by example how if you acquire a set of usable skills it is possible to remain consistently employed with a degree in anthropology in academic and nonacademic settings. Fifth, I use the story to highlight a number of important characteristics involved in working as an anthropologist in diverse settings, namely, broad research interests, flexibility, creativity, and a willingness to work under a series of different job titles. Having used my own story to set the tone for the class, I then encourage students to go forth and create their own stories in which they put their anthropological education to use.

Textbox I.1.2.   Autobiographical Account by Amy Goldmacher

My undergraduate degree was in anthropology, because I was fascinated by why people behaved the way they did. When I graduated from college, I knew I wasn't ready for graduate school, and I wanted to work in industry to get some money and experience.

My first real job was with an academic publishing company in Boston. I started at the lowest level as an editorial assistant. For the first time, I had a steady paycheck, benefits, a cubicle, a boss, and steady, regular work hours. I moved into the marketing department after two years, where I worked with the retail sales force on how to position some of our textbooks in nonacademic stores. Two years later, I took a position as a sales representative in Los Angeles because I had always wanted to live in California and a sales rep position was essential to being promoted within the company. My job consisted of going to see professors in their offices on college campuses and discussing the textbooks they would require in their courses. I felt like I was doing anthropology as I saw the "natives" in their local environments and tried to understand their textbook needs. Being a sales rep reminded me of what I liked about anthropology, because I was working with people and trying to collect information and provide solutions. My job experiences inspired me to look for graduate programs that would increase those skills and allow me to return to industry with the credentials and experience to provide assessments and consultation services in organizational settings. At the time, Wayne State University in Detroit offered the only Ph.D. in anthropology with a specialization in business anthropology in the United States, so my choice of graduate school was relatively easy.

As a full-time graduate student, I work part time as a research assistant in the Department of Industrial and Manufacturing Engineering. This department realizes the value of the anthropological approach to engineering projects in the automotive industry, so I am receiving practical experience and exposure in industry, which is preparing me for my career after graduate school. I may not be hired for a job called "anthropologist," but the variety of my work experience allows me to demonstrate how the methods and theories of anthropology are relevant.

It is our desire that you use this book's exercises to be able to tell your own story in a similar manner. By doing the exercises, you can reflect on your own anthropological education and personal experiences, reenvision your skill set, and cast a wider net in the job market. Hopefully, you will choose to go over this exercise process again at different times as you design your anthropological career.

2

Positioning Yourself in the Discipline

Creating Your Anthropological Career and Overcoming Challenges

As mentioned in the previous chapter, anthropology is a broad social science that looks at many different aspects of the human experience through time and across space. The holistic and comparative orientation of the field—and the ways in which we examine the complex relationships between culture, biology, social organization, and language—makes it well suited to engage with fundamental questions about what it means to be human. Numerous anthropology textbooks and other resources do a good job of orienting students to the content of each of the subfields as well as how they relate to one another. You should make sure you have a grasp of this fundamental subject matter before trying to position yourself in the discipline.

Anthropologists are also well recognized for their expertise in areas such as studying culture, human diversity, and ethnographic methods. Nowadays we are often called upon to use these skills as well as many others in a wide variety of work settings. Although anthropology was often associated in the past with in-depth fieldwork in small-scale societies, the professional roles for anthropologists have greatly broadened. Indeed, as mentioned earlier, there are many anthropologists now working on large-scale problems in numerous complex settings such as international development agencies, healthcare organizations, and global corporations. Further, the methods of our discipline are now more widely recognized for their relevance and are even frequently borrowed by those from other fields, such as in business or design (see Table I.2.1).

These examples illustrate that there are opportunities for you to work as an anthropologist in any number of settings and make a valuable contribution drawing upon your training. You may have just declared anthropology as your major, or you may be graduating with your BA in anthropology. Perhaps you are contemplating a graduate degree in anthropology or looking

Table I.2.1.   Examples of Fields in Which Professional Anthropologists Work

Field	Illustration of Job Activity
Community development	Outreach activities, program design, and/or evaluation
Government	Implement and analyze policies and programs
Archaeology	Document and explain the origins and development of human cultures through examination of material remains
Museums	Interpret and manage material culture collections
Linguistics	Study social uses of language
Business	Research customers, processes, and/or products
Health	Assess health knowledge, risk behavior, and/or health education
Forensics	Identify human remains to assist in the detection of crime

to complement your current field with anthropology. Whatever the case, we recommend envisioning what you ultimately want to be doing to help you plan how to get there. Working backward from your goal will ensure that you take the steps to achieve it. Additionally, being more familiar with what you can do and would like to do can also help you recognize unexpected career opportunities as they arise.

Up until now, much of what has been written on the roles of theory and practice in the discipline has too frequently focused on carving out the respective territories of academic, applied, and practicing anthropology. Of course, definitions are usually much neater than the real world application. In the simplest terms, academic anthropology was traditionally thought of as generating knowledge, and practicing anthropology was considered to be applying knowledge or providing solutions to problems (Ervin 2004). In this conceptual scheme, one can envision a continuum with academic anthropology at one end and practicing anthropology at the other. Bridging these areas is a middle ground called *applied anthropology*. Here we find the practical application of knowledge generated through theory and basic research that comes from an academic setting. Table I.2.2 gives some examples of the types of work that would be done by academic, applied, and practicing anthropologists.

Table I.2.2.   One View of Academic, Applied, and Practicing Anthropology

Academic anthropologist	A college or university professor who primarily teaches, researches, and publishes, drawing from and contributing to the theoretical knowledge in the field
Applied anthropologist	A college or university professor who researches and consults on projects outside of academia in addition to academic responsibilities
Practicing anthropologist	A self-employed agent or employee of an organization who works on projects guided by the employer's needs

Since the conceptual scheme presented here is well known in the field today, most students are keenly interested in figuring out where the kinds of work they want to do fall along this continuum and what it takes to be successful in that area. An academic anthropologist is usually classified as someone who works in a university setting, doing activities such as teaching, writing grants, conducting research, and publishing. When academic anthropologists are evaluated, their use of and contribution to anthropological theory is considered very important. An applied anthropologist may also be housed in a university and engaged in teaching, research, and publishing. However, his or her research and other work activities, such as advocacy or consulting, frequently involve organizations or clients outside the university setting. In judging the work of applied anthropologists, factors such as community impact and community service are heavily weighted. Practicing anthropologists are a broader and more eclectic category. They may be employed by various agencies on a long- or short-term basis, they may be self-employed, or contractors, or may be full-time employees of organizations. They can be doing a wide variety of activities including research, training, consulting, program evaluation, or policy making. Because this is a diverse group doing varied activities, their employment arrangements and how they are judged may also be more variable (Nolan 2003, p. 6). Keep in mind that the majority of jobs for anthropologists will be in this third category, and that you may or may not be working under the job title anthropologist here. Pay scale is also likely to be the widest in this third category, as it can include a continuum from voluntary to low-paying to high-paying jobs. In the academic world, salaries are generally more consistent and assigned by academic rank (e.g., assistant versus associate professor), although there can still be some variation here as well.

Regrettably, a "schism between academic and practicing anthropology" exists (Hill 2000, p. 3). Traditionally, anthropology was known for its four main subfields: cultural anthropology, physical anthropology, linguistics, and archaeology. Whether applied anthropology is a subpart of each of the four subfields or a fifth subfield of its own is a topic that has been extensively discussed in the field (for some examples just since 2000, see Ervin 2004, Ferraro 2008, Gwynne 2003, Hill 2000, Kedia & van Willigen 2005, Lamphere 2004, Nolan 2003, Omohundro 2001, 2007, and van Willigen 2002). We invite you to use these references as a starting point to investigate this debate yourself.

To some, the divide between academic anthropology and the more applied or practicing branches of the field means that "anthropological practice remains the poor relation within the discipline" (Nolan 2003, p. 22). Part of the problem may be that academic and applied anthropology have often been viewed as having different priorities, objectives, and outcomes (Hill 2000, p. 7). The following quote well illustrates how some in the field have characterized this division. Although academic and applied anthropology both seek to conceptualize human problems, academic anthropology "increase[s] and disseminate[s] knowledge in the field" and applied anthropology "alleviate[s] human suffering or injustice or redefine[s] . . . issues" (Hill 2000, p. 7). Too often the debate in the field continues to be presented in overly simplistic terms; however, there is much interest in moving the discussion forward and better addressing the true complexities of the situation. On a hopeful note, Louise Lamphere, a past president of the American Anthropological Association, wrote the following in 2004:

> At a time when some of our colleagues are still decrying the disunity of our discipline, there are signs of increased unity and the potential for increased communication across subfields as we look for better strategies for collaboration, outreach, and advocacy. There is still much work to be done, particularly in institutionalizing techniques for collaboration, outreach and policy research as part of our graduate training. Nevertheless, the current sea change within the discipline suggests that anthropology is and will continue to become a more respected, better known, and unified discipline. (p. 440).

We agree that the field as a whole is moving in the right direction in this regard. However, it is important for you to still know about the issues summarized above, because even though we, as do many others, believe this distinction between academic and applied or practicing anthropology is an artificial divide, you will likely be viewed and categorized as one of the above as you progress through your training. We anticipate that in the future, these false boundaries will recede further, but for now you need to operate in the world as it is and therefore be familiar with this major disciplinary debate. To cut a long story short, keep in mind that all of these approaches can be highly complementary. At the same time be aware of what the categorical schemes operating in the field are and think about how to position yourself, rather than simply being labeled by others.

The State of Anthropology Education Today

An anthropology education that combines traditional disciplinary topics with contemporary career preparation will help prepare you to succeed both in our society and the world at large. We live in an increasingly connected world where complex cultural, historical, economic, organizational, and political processes all shape social relations and policy formation. Take a minute to start to think about what the implications of this re-ality may be for your own work life in the future. As has been mentioned before, the breadth of our training and our ability to take holistic and comparative perspectives make anthropologists well suited to work on important twenty-first-century issues. Although standard topics in an-thropological education, such as understanding cross-cultural variation and appreciating human diversity, remain important cornerstones of the discipline, it is increasingly recognized that this classic education alone is not adequate to build a career when a student leaves the university with an anthropology degree. Rather there is a need to better prepare anthro-pology students academically, professionally, and personally to take on the new complex roles awaiting them upon degree completion.

Although there is growing interest in better addressing these impor-tant learning objectives, you need to know more about the state of anthro-pological education today to figure out what gaps may exist in your own knowledge, skills, and training. Nowadays various anthropology depart-ments often classify themselves as offering four- or five-field curricula. Re-lated to this categorization scheme, they may promote themselves and be viewed by others as "traditional academic" or "applied" programs. Al-though these labels are used all the time by those in the field, much more needs to be done to clearly link how each of these stances explicitly relates to the types of education and career development activities provided in these departments. Although a department may view its own mission as primarily producing either academics or practitioners, how the educa-tional objectives within various courses fit together with explicit career preparation activities and gaining specific skills is often much less clearly defined.

Concern over how anthropology programs prepare students for ca-reers, especially outside of academia, has been expressed since the late 1970s. In a survey conducted of anthropologists working in the private sector in the early 1980s, Marietta Baba found specific areas of knowledge recommended by practitioners as necessary for anthropology program graduates who wished to find employment outside of academia. These knowledge areas include among others "having competency in social science research techniques, the ability to work in cross-disciplinary or cross-functional teams, quantitative skills, communication skills, and com-petency in related substantive fields" (Baba 1986, pp. 22–25). Such skills are still critically needed and wanted by anthropology graduates several decades later, but more remains to be done to move these areas more squarely into the academic curriculum in many anthropology programs. There has been some good dialogue in the field about how to move in this direction. To give just one example here, Lamphere's article mentioned above provides a thoughtful discussion of how to extend students' training in collaboration, outreach, and policy activities while they are in school (Lamphere 2004).

In addition to classroom-based education, additional opportunities must be made available in the academic curriculum for more experiential education. In work settings, applying anthropology is a process that often involves turning implicit knowledge into explicit practice. More places need to exist in the academic anthropology curriculum where students can practice turning classroom knowledge into relevant job skills. Although you may do well in a course, how do you demonstrate to a potential employer what that course means in terms of acquired experience, critical thinking, problem-solving skills, and value in the workplace? How do the skills of anthropologists complement those of other disciplines? And even more basic may be the attempt to explain to others not knowledgeable about the field what anthropology education is and why it is useful. You will be using the exercises in this book as an instructive process for answering some of these questions regarding your own situation.

Why are the linkages between academic learning and practical skills more critical than ever in anthropology education these days? A growing trend is that more jobs for anthropology graduates at all levels, including those with Ph.D.s, will not be in academia. A major issue is that the academic job market has, since the mid-1970s, not been able to keep up with the number of anthropologists graduating with Ph.D.s, and anthropologists have had to look outside academia for jobs (Ferraro 2008). In addition, new career opportunities have been created in different realms outside of academia as well. For example, more federal legislation requiring policy research has added a variety of new jobs for which anthropologists are well suited (Ferraro 2008). This present-day employment reality is not bad if anthropology students are better prepared to work in other areas.

Although such major employment shifts occurred in the field, many anthropology departments did not modify their curricula accordingly. As a result, there is much current debate over how well anthropology departments meet the needs of their students. Some have even strongly argued that "a glaring mismatch exists between anthropology graduate programs in the United States and the careers of their graduates" (Price 2001, p. 55). For instance, some anthropology departments still struggle with their orientation to applied anthropology and whether to offer applied degree programs or applied components within traditional four-field academic programs. Even where such coursework and degree programs are now routinely offered, there is still considerable discussion about what the standards are for judging rigor in an area of the field. This perceived lack of across-the-board standards is somewhat surprising considering that other disciplines have managed to handle incorporation of their applied branches and related educational processes more smoothly. Where these assessment issues have been addressed most comprehensively in our field is in the university departments that have created specific degree programs in applied anthropology. However, an ongoing problem for these departments is to be recognized as within the mainstream of the field rather than as their own specific subbranch. Although students are "asking for applied courses and 'mainstream' courses with applied and experiential components" (Simonelli 2001), the reality is that these offerings are quite limited in many programs. Troublingly, "few anthropology graduates are trained specifically for the demands of practice" and

> the result is that most anthropology graduates—unlike, say, their counterparts in business, medicine, law, or engineering—enter the job market underprepared for the challenges and opportunities that await them. Instead, with a few notable exceptions, anthropological training in the United States prepares students primarily as academics. (Nolan 2003, p. x)

What is clearly needed are more opportunities for anthropology students to put their educational backgrounds to use earlier on, and these students will need situations where they can practice doing anthropology and using their knowledge of anthropology's history, theories, and methods. Although some in the discipline have passionately spoken out about these needs for quite a long time, the field as a whole is now paying greater attention to these vital educational issues. It is widely recognized within the discipline that anthropology graduates have a lot to offer, and it is increasingly obvious that more needs to be done to ensure that they are able to communicate these abilities to others outside our disciplinary realm. Therefore, beyond what you learn in anthropology classes, you will likely have to do some extra work on your own. Specifically, you must explicitly think about how your formal academic education has prepared you for using anthropology in your work life, the strengths and limitations of your current training, and what additional career development activities you need to engage in to round out your background. Importantly, you need to learn how to communicate the value of an anthropologist's broad generalist background to others and convince them that your combination of skills can be a major asset in their workplace. You need to be able to coherently and convincingly make this case without ever being apologetic for being an anthropologist.

More teaching and learning resources on anthropological career preparation that handle this crucial subject in creative and hands-on ways are also needed. Although this topic is frequently given some space in applied anthropology textbooks, it is mainly written about descriptively, and students just read this information. But in our opinion, students should be actively engaged in this area instead of having a more passive interaction, such as a reading assignment. In other words, it is like the difference between attending a lecture and doing a project yourself. Whereas you can definitely learn from both formats, one is much more hands-on than the other. We think the active learning style in which students have to do something is generally better when it comes to career preparation activities and makes it easier to personalize the circumstances, which is necessary. Hence, the exercises in this book are designed to make the learning experience very real and practical for you.

In summary, this section has provided some background information about the state of anthropology education today as it particularly relates to career preparation. We have indicated that along with learning to use reasoning and approaches from the four traditional fields of anthropology and how to apply this knowledge to addressing real world issues, there is a definite need for more formal career training while in school. Specifically, the education of contemporary anthropologists must include, in addition to solid academic preparation, a career training component that provides the tools to be able to find relevant jobs (including those not necessarily labeled "anthropologist") and the language to be able to communicate how and why you are well-trained and well-suited for these jobs. Students need to know about the different avenues in which they can work as an anthropologist, and they must become familiar with these various pathways while in school to make informed choices about career options, acquire proper training for their chosen area, and then be able to present themselves to nonanthropologist audiences as well.

Taking a Life Course Perspective on Your Anthropological Career

The life course is a powerful concept for thinking about the culture-specific ways in which the stages, activities, and transitions in individuals' lives and the social lives of groups occur. (For more background on the history of this concept, see Fortes 1971, Fry 2003, Mortimer and Shanahan 2006, Settersten 2003, Turner 1969, and Van Gennep 1960.) For anthropologists, it may not be surprising to hear that there are social expectations concerning appropriate behavior and work at different ages and stages of life in every culture. A useful concept for thinking about what are considered to be "normal" patterns of behavior is the *social clock*. These social clocks bring people to say things like "I married late in life" or "I'm a nontraditional student." What is viewed as "late" or "nontraditional" is indeed shaped by culturally constructed frameworks. Those who study the anthropology of aging have used this concept to discuss whether people perceive they are in synch with certain responsibilities and expectations that they associate with particular life stages.

The good news is that while everyone knows about these social clocks in their own society, they do not need to restrict the development of your career path. Meaning, you may feel pressures to make certain career decisions, but anthropologically, you recognize that these pressures are culturally constructed. Once you recognize the pressures for what they are, you have the freedom to work around them. On the one hand, you certainly need to be aware of these social clocks in order to understand how potential employers and others may perceive your own anthropological career path. However, think back to what you learned about the transmission of cultural knowledge in your introductory anthropology class. Although cultural beliefs, values, and expectations are often widely learned and shared, culture is also adaptable and can transform over time. Thus, while individuals may know about broad cultural patterns regarding work life and "typical" career trajectories, they are not bound by a certain set of "rules" that restrict them from doing things differently. There is both inter- and intragroup variation in how people structure their lives. Also, cultural notions about what appropriate life trajectories are and how life events should be timed can and do change over time. Think about different generations of your own family members; for instance, when their formal education began and ended, their ages of marriage, when they left home, the length of time they stayed at the same job, and so forth. When you make some of these comparisons, you will begin to see how culture can and does change over time. Thus, it can be very freeing to know that while certain social conventions may exist regarding current perceptions of work life, you can feel at liberty to deviate from them if it suits you. Who knows, maybe in a couple of decades your way of doing things will seem more mainstream!

Another relevant point to make here is that ideas about work in the twenty-first century are changing, and people are working longer, and in more settings, than ever before, and people are not necessarily retiring. Trends such as less job security, underemployment, more competition for jobs, and more career changes over time have all resulted in a need to rethink what work means to people over their life courses (Gamst 1995). A significant perk is that the nonlinear career path may provide greater flexibility to navigate and make changes in direction. This aspect can indeed be critical in having a fulfilling work life over time.

So the question then is what broader ideas should you take away from this discussion about taking a life course perspective to your work life? You may just be starting out and anthropology is your first career, or you may be returning to the workforce, or shifting fields entirely. As you develop your anthropological career, there are several messages we wish to convey relating to taking a life course approach. First, it is important to be aware of social clocks but never let them wholly determine your choices about what you can do at each stage of your life. Of course it may be easier or more difficult to get particular types of jobs at certain ages or stages of life. Picture the following scenario, for instance: maybe you have retired from your first career as a high school English teacher, studied anthropology, and now you want to join the Peace Corps and teach English overseas. Although your anthropology background and life experience may be well suited for this type of work, you may have certain health issues that prevent you from passing a required physical examination for the Peace Corps, or perhaps family demands prevent you from leaving the United States for an extended period of time. However, maybe you could work for another agency or teach English as a second language in the United States. The point here is that you have valuable life and work experiences and you can make a meaningful contribution in your chosen area. There are always multiple ways to reach your goals; be flexible and willing to consider different avenues and different timing for getting there.

Second, when taking a life course approach to your career it can be very reassuring to believe in the viewpoint that *it all gets used*. What we mean by this statement is that you need to trust that you will be able to take your diverse life and work experiences and figure out over time how they inform one another and have made you into the person you are today. As our personal work histories presented earlier show, you can take a series of seemingly unrelated jobs and create a coherent anthropological career out of your eclectic background. Although we know from firsthand experience that doing this is highly possible, it will require you to highlight for potential employers how your prior skills and broad general background will be a significant advantage in their particular work situations. In other words, it is up to you to tell the story of your work experiences in a clear way that makes sense to someone hearing this story for the first time. Let's use the metaphor of weaving here to further illustrate. Your goal is to weave together the threads of your background and hopefully create a beautiful tapestry out of it, however large or small it may be. This tapestry with all of its intricate and different threads is your masterpiece, and you should be proud of how you have woven it together over time. It may not have been created in a linear or orderly fashion; it may include sections that you ripped out and rewove into a different pattern. When you subscribe to the viewpoint *it all gets used*, you will realize that you can always become more proficient and improve your weaving over time. Our exercises will help you practice weaving together the threads of your current background and demonstrate how to actively live in this mode. The truth of the matter is that not every employer will fully appreciate the beauty of the woven tapestry that is your career or what it may show about your weaving capabilities. Keep in mind that not every work of art is well suited for hanging in every space. However, if you have confidence that *it all gets used*, you will incorporate what you learn through the weaving process and be resilient, fold up your masterpiece, and take it somewhere else where it is more likely to be valued.

Over time, anthropologists have blazed career trails and done what might have seemed unusual or impossible before, entering new realms where this type of hire was never previously considered. Some anthropologists even had jobs created especially for them, based on their particular skills. Hearing their stories about how they got these jobs can be very insightful as you are getting started and in later stages of career development as well. It is likely that someone has created a career path similar to what you want to do, so the networks and communities of established anthropologists and colleagues are great resources for up-and-coming anthropologists.

Everyone can benefit from good mentorship. We believe that it is most advantageous to have multiple mentors. These can be anthropologists and nonanthropologists; a mentor can be anyone whose judgment you trust and advice you seek. A mentor can both encourage and constructively critique your ideas and work. Mentors can be people who are in your personal life or your professional life, or cross over these domains. The concept here is to be able to get a range of input from diverse people who do not all think in similar ways or even value or prioritize the same things. Inevitably, if you have a variety of mentors, they may offer conflicting advice about what choices you should make or what you should do in specific circumstances. The mentors will be able to see your strengths and weaknesses, your skills acquired and skills needed, and good opportunities as well as ones that are not as promising. You must then take all of this feedback and decide what to do with it, but you will be better equipped to do so from getting this mixture of perspectives. We have an exercise later in the book that will enable you to further contemplate roles and expectations for mentoring relationships that you would like to have. We strongly encourage you to share all of your responses to all the exercises with your mentors. The exercises can help you discuss a series of important career-related topics in a more structured way and help you get additional valuable feedback.

Another important benefit of good mentoring is that your mentors can help you to develop a strong professional network. They can introduce you to new people, and if you have a range of mentors, it can be expected that they will know different people as well. Oftentimes the mentor can serve as a liaison to meeting people and as an advocate who puts in a good word about you and your capabilities as well. Like mentoring, networking involves finding people you can learn from and help. Your mentors can aid you with learning to communicate effectively in such situations. Some of the exercises will help you with introducing yourself and communicating about your interests, skill set, and what you can offer. Keep in mind that networking is an important ongoing career activity and not just something you do when you are job hunting.

In summary, we have shown how using a life course approach is beneficial for envisioning and reenvisioning your work life over time. Just because you have chosen a more unusual, less linear anthropological career path is no reason to be discouraged or dissuaded from it, whatever age or stage of life you are in. The exercises will help you think about how to draw upon your valuable life experiences that can be a significant asset in the workplace. The message from this section is that while one needs to be aware of social and cultural influences on your career aspirations, do not let them dictate your path. Instead, be at the helm of your own decision making and consciously use what you know about social clocks as only part of a broader assessment of the employment landscape and your own opportunities. Given that anthropology is still a path less trodden, you will have to do some hard thinking about how this career path or career transition fits in with what is going on in the rest of your life and your short- and long-term goals.

Overcoming the Challenges in Creating an Anthropology Career

Although there are more jobs today for which anthropologists are well suited, not everyone is advertising to hire an anthropologist or necessarily aware that hiring someone with anthropological training could be beneficial. These facts are not easy to accept, but coming to terms with these realities sooner rather than later will help you to strategize how to best overcome these issues. Oftentimes, after working with an anthropologist, an employer may be much more willing to do so again, having seen first-hand the contributions that an anthropological perspective can make. Make sure to network with those who have already been successful at breaking down these barriers and find out how they did it. Figuring out how they became and remained employed will likely yield some valuable insights that you can incorporate into your own job-seeking strategy. There are many anthropologists who have successfully traveled this path before you and are willing to share their experiences. Keep in mind that everyone's path is individual and no one said this undertaking is easy. Despite the challenges, following your heart where your career is concerned can make achieving your goals so much sweeter. In the end, you will probably be more fulfilled and rewarded by doing something you truly love.

A second challenge is that you may not be well compensated, especially compared to colleagues in other fields where the pay scale may be considerably higher. These financial issues are not universal: some specialties such as business anthropology may more often provide opportunities to do lucrative consulting work and command a higher salary than other anthropological specialties. There are, however, many areas of anthropology, such as community outreach work in the nonprofit sector, where resources may be much more limited, and it is not possible to expect to be paid at a level similar to for-profit work. Yet that is still no reason to accept unreasonably low pay! It is critical to be informed, to know what is possible, what the pay is like for similar positions, and what you can ask for.

Additionally, it is important to realize that you are consciously making personal choices for your career: how interesting the project is and to what extent it is a stepping-stone to something else that you may want to do for intellectual reasons, social justice, future financial gain, or access to other opportunities, to name a few. We know a very talented anthropology student with a high-paying blue-collar job in another field wishing to make a career transition (both out of love for anthropology and changes in his present industry) who stated in frustration and anger, "What bill did anthropology ever pay for me?" It would be irresponsible not to mention this financial dilemma for a few reasons. First, this concern is one of the largest overall worries that those studying anthropology face. Making the transition to anthropology may mean financial insecurity, if you are giving up a paying job to go back to school, or to change from a field where you have industry experience and command a high salary to start over in anthropology. Second, it would be particularly hypocritical for us not to discuss this issue up front since this book is written by authors at a large public university in a state that has recently faced much economic turmoil. In our setting, many students are working people who are paying for their own education and expecting to see some significant gain from it.

We cannot say that the gain will or will not always be financial. An anthropology education may have a beneficial economic result, or the main benefit may be the opportunity to transition into a more rewarding line of work. An anthropology education may provide great intellectual challenge and social justice opportunities, to leave the world a better place than you found it. We cannot tell you whether your investment in anthropology is ultimately worthwhile for you—that is a highly personal matter to consider. All we can do here is provide some structured ways to think about these issues and help you make your choices in more conscious and informed ways. Because we take a life course approach, the factors that weigh in your decisions may vary at different moments in your life: how badly do you want to be an anthropologist, is it worth it to you monetarily, does your current financial and life situation allow you to do it? This book will allow you to reuse our decision-making tools so that you can continuously explore your career options or revisit the tools at different decision-making times in your career. As we demonstrated in the previous chapter by telling our own stories, we do know that it is possible to be employed and be employed consistently using your anthropological skills, whether you are called an anthropologist or not! You need to be self-motivated, creative, flexible, and willing to think out of the box to find these opportunities. To sum up, be optimistic, be realistic, be open-minded.

3

How to Use This Book Effectively

This book is meant to be something different from an applied anthropology textbook or a generic career preparation book that simply tells you the steps of how to write your resumé. Whereas numerous books like that already exist, what we think is missing from our field is a more self-directed career exploration workbook for anthropologists that more fully addresses career development at different stages as well as first-time job hunting. Our agenda was to produce such a resource, and this project has truly been a labor of love for us. We really want you to feel empowered to use your education to work anthropologically, regardless of what you are actually being called or paid to do. If our advice and exercises help you to establish yourself and find meaningful work, we will be very satisfied.

We encourage you to also take advantage of the standard career services of your institution (e.g., resumé preparation, job interview training). At the same time, you should understand that these services are typically designed for more conventional career paths. Make sure that you go beyond your own institution's career center and also get input from anthropologists about your materials as well about how to best package and present a nonlinear career background. Developing relationships through the national professional anthropology associations can be very useful. You can search the websites of major anthropology associations (American Anthropological Association [AAA] at www.aaanet.org, Society for Applied Anthropology [SfAA] at www.sfaa.net, and National Association for the Practice of Anthropology [NAPA] at www.practicinganthropology.org to name just three) for ways to connect with anthropologists who share your interests. There are often listservs to subscribe to, which will provide you with a community of people to interact with and from whom you can seek advice, or blogs to read, or electronic communities to join. See what you can find that's already out there to suit your needs!

Finally, it is important to recognize that nobody has all of the answers, including how to conduct the best job search, obtain the most perfect starting job, and build the finest career. Rather, people will do things in their own way. Developing a career is an ongoing and creative activity. Your job searching strategy will be your own. What we know from designing our own careers is the following: just as when you read a novel, you will envision the characters in your own way, so it will be with these exercises. We look forward to that personalization occurring. Because when such processes happen, we know that we have achieved our main educational goals in writing this book: that you have used these materials in a way that makes sense for you and made them your own.

Exercise Process and Format

Let's move on to talking about how to effectively do the exercises. The fifteen exercises that follow are arranged thematically. First, the "Understanding Yourself as an Anthropologist" exercises will help you develop and articulate your preferences, your personal and professional histories, and your abilities that can translate well across fields into specific work-related skills. Most importantly, these exercises will prompt you to both think about and develop the appropriate language for conveying what is anthropological about your experiences to date and as your career moves forward. The "Representing Yourself Professionally as an Anthropologist" exercises entail thinking about how you can best communicate your anthropological abilities through career-related materials. You will be able to use these materials in your current job searches, and you will be able to adapt them as your career advances. All of the exercises take the life course perspective that we discussed earlier in order to help you envision and reenvision your anthropological career trajectory over time.

There are several levels at which you can engage in these exercises. Ideally, you will approach them thoughtfully and do them at different points in your career trajectory over the course of your life. Your needs will change over time, as will your insights. Think about using this book as though it were exercise equipment at a gym. In order to get the full benefit of weight training, you need to establish a routine and keep doing it. You will need to increase your weights to see results. The same principle is true with these career exercises: if you rush through them and write up something quickly without reflecting deeply on the topic, you won't receive the same benefit you would if you had devoted your time and energy to them. These exercises will help you do for yourself what a life coach or career counselor might charge you to do!

The exercises are arranged in a particular order that we think makes sense for either a class to use or as an individually guided process. Although you will most likely initially do the exercises on your own, it can then be very useful to come together and discuss them in a group setting, such as in an anthropology class or career club. In this way, you can get others' valuable feedback about what steps or actions to take next. We have seen at Wayne State that students often provide new and helpful insights to other classmates to further sharpen their own thinking about how to proceed with designing their career strategies. If you reuse these exercises at different moments in your career (and we hope that you do), you may then be working on your own. Both doing the exercises solo and in a group are useful, but it can certainly be beneficial to go through the process for the first time with others. Also, let's be real: it is easier to be motivated to get things done well and on time if someone is expecting you to show up having completed these exercises and being ready to discuss them together. Like everything else in life, the outcome of what you get out of doing these exercises will greatly depend on the effort you put into them.

You do not have to systematically go through the exercises in the order we arranged them. Some exercises may seem most relevant to your situation now. You may be short on time, or patience, or have a job interview tomorrow! Accordingly, you can work through the exercises in any order that makes sense for you. However, some of the concepts in the exercises build on a previous concept. The best thing to do is to view the entire process as an ongoing opportunity for personal growth; as you encounter related themes in later exercises, don't simply repeat what you wrote before. Challenge yourself to view the material in a new way, build upon what you wrote before, and take it further—it will only benefit you in the end.

Each exercise is formatted in the following way:

Activity Overview: Describes the point of the exercise, what you will be doing, and what you can expect to learn.

Instructions: Tells you step-by-step specifically how to do the exercise and includes samples, prompts, or suggestions to aid you in the process of creating something that's unique to you.

Self-Reflection: Asks you to contemplate what the process of doing a particular exercise was like for you and envision what might be different if you were to do the same exercise at a different time in your life or career.

Follow-Up Activities: Suggests activities you can do afterward to reinforce your learning, prepare for specific situations (e.g., rehearsing for a job interview), or take the exercise one step further in your life.

Each of the fifteen exercises in Part II is followed by a sample written by a student. We include examples from undergraduate, MA, and Ph.D. students to show a range of experience levels, approaches to the task, and points of view. We hope that you will find these samples instructive in thinking about how to get started, regardless of whether the person writing the sample is at a similar educational or experiential stage as you, or at a different moment in his or her career trajectory and/or life course. Some of the samples are longer than others; some are written in the exact way the exercise is presented or even copied from the body of the exercise, others use the exercise format as a jumping-off point and take the exercise in their own direction. We hope these illustrate ways in which you can approach the exercises, but we want you to draw on your own creativity and experience in order to get the most out of them.

Storing Your Materials

We encourage you to save all of your materials from doing the exercises in an organized fashion. You can use any type of storage system that works well for you. Your storage system could be very low tech, such as paper folders in a filing cabinet. This way of doing things enables you to easily file other related items, such as newspaper clippings, as you come across them over time. Alternatively, you may prefer to store your personal data electronically, such as in a hand-held organizer, memory stick, or on your computer. In this day and age, the benefits and convenience of having your files accessible and portable are obvious. Please keep in mind that this book takes a life course approach to your career, which means we are interested in your job search now and how you may return to use these materials again at later points in your career. All forms of technology soon become outdated. Make sure that you keep transferring this information or printing out hard copies so that your information will be available to you long after you have updated your word processing software or transitioned to a different computer. We also recommend regularly backing up the files on your computer and making sure that you also have them stored on nonmagnetic media as well. If anything should happen to your primary storage device (like your only personal computer), you will have a hard copy and an electronic version stored elsewhere. We hope that you will never have to use your backups, but it's better to be safe than sorry!

The bottom line here is to devise a well-thought-out long-term strategy for keeping track of this critical personal information. You will see sooner or later that there is almost no such thing as being too careful or overplanning in this area. Whether your system involves storing copies of your notes and jottings from doing the exercises in a fireproof safe, or another building, or a bank vault, or on the Internet, just plan ahead. There are heartbreaking stories of people needing to find jobs following devastating hurricanes or other disasters who do not have any of their documents available to create a new resumé. Of course, you can re-create these items, but do you really want to have to do so in a crisis situation?

The reality, however, is that most people who lose some or all of their essential personal documents will do so in much more ordinary and mundane ways. An example is storing this key information in packing boxes that get lost when you move, when you could have put them in your car with your most valuable possessions. Just as you would not want to lose something as precious as photographs from earlier in your life, treat your own writings and thoughts in the same manner. If you have stowed your things carefully and backed up your documents properly, it will not be a problem if you move and some of your boxes are lost. This information will exist elsewhere. We are writing about these issues not to scare you, but to impress upon you the tremendous value of giving some thought to how you store your vital personal information. Here, we are talking specifically about career preparation documents, but the point is relevant for other important areas of life as well.

The truth is that time passes very quickly for all of us and if you do not adequately document your thinking about career issues over time, you may well wish that you had done so. Here are some examples from other parts of life that are apt metaphors: maybe you were meaning to take a picture of your puppy or kitten before they were full grown or your children before they were walking, yet if you do not document these very important stages, you cannot go back and do it after the critical time has passed. No one ever has enough time in their daily lives, but we urge you to pay attention and take care of these important activities when it makes sense to do so. For instance, think about these issues during times of changes like graduation, switching jobs, or shifting career directions.

Of course, the whole discussion about carefully storing your personal documents is supposed to be preemptive. Hopefully, you have begun to see from this discussion what a great resource these exercises can be for analyzing changes in your thinking and career strategy over time. These materials are very useful in writing resumés, personal statements for graduate school, job presentations, and so forth. Indeed, having these documents will enable you to trace shifts in your thinking, how you came to focus on new areas, and build up certain domains of knowledge and ex-perience. In short, you will be able to see how you became the person you are today, which can be a very empowering and useful process. When you are consciously aware of these processes, you are likely to be able to better communicate to others how you became the person you are with the skills you have.

However you store your materials, make sure they are easily accessi-ble and that all of your documents are dated. Keeping track of these ver-sions will help you to see how your thinking may have changed over time. As indicated above, reading your older accounts can provide interesting insights later on when you are revisiting your job-seeking strategy or changing lines of work or your area of emphasis. Dating or creating ver-sions all of your documents will also help you to locate the most recent ones without difficulty when it is time to write a cover letter, update your resumé, and so on. For example, we saved versions of this book with a name and date in the filename (such as Book Front Section 030408.doc) so that every time we made a change, we renamed the document with the current date, so all previous versions were sorted chronologically in our electronic files. This way we could easily access the most current version as well as go back to older versions for material (see Textbox I.3.1).

Textbox I.3.1. Two Examples of Using and Reusing Exercises to Help You Move Forward

Scenario 1
You initially did these exercises as a traditional undergraduate student, then you graduated and worked in your first full-time job for several years. Now you have decided to go to graduate school and you need to write a personal statement for an admission application describing your education, back-ground, research interests, and anticipated career path. If you have kept your documents well organized, you will be well on your way to doing this task ef-ficiently and effectively.

Scenario 2
You are going on a job interview and want to revisit your job-seeking strategy over time. You can more easily plan what you are going to say if you can read-ily find your materials from doing these exercises. By referring to the content in your old exercises, you can craft a story that describes your past job expe-riences. You'll be surprised at the varied purposes these materials are used over time. Case in point: we had to dig out some of our materials from earlier on to write our own personal work histories for this book!

To sum up, getting organized and storing your materials carefully are important investments in yourself. Please take this process seriously and plan ahead as you are getting started with the exercises. Having your old notes and being able to review your writings from the first time you did the career exercises can help you to use your prior train of thought as a jumping off point for what you are considering now. If you are contemplating a midcareer change, for instance, you may use your earlier writings to trace how your thinking has changed over time and what you've learned along the way. We have become tedious with endlessly talking about backing things up, so just remember that you can't get your thoughts back again as easily as you can replace other material possessions from your life. Enough said—just do it!

Getting Feedback and Hearing from You

As we explained earlier, a good number of the exercises were designed for and used in anthropology courses at Wayne State University over the past six years. Having seen students interact with these assignments, the different ways in which they have approached doing the tasks with their own diverse learning styles has been fascinating. This process has also resulted in nearly all of the exercises being modified, sometimes significantly, over time. The exercises and related instructions have frequently been made more open-ended and flexible. What we learned over time was that students demonstrated different preferences for working with the same career planning concepts. To give just one brief example here, a very visually oriented artistic student chose to make an elaborate layered collage rather than write a narrative statement about how she envisioned both the specific parts and overall direction of her career. The message for us teaching this material was that students will approach the task at hand in their own ways. Some may want to write out their answers; others have different creative ways of expressing their thoughts. So please feel free to think and work as it suits your style.

Indeed, we would be very interested in hearing about various creative ways in which you used the exercises. You, as a user of the exercises, will know whether the exercises are helpful, practical, and worth investing your valuable time to do them. We all know that students are chronically busy, juggling many different assignments and types of demands. With that in mind, we want to make a workbook that is really helpful and constructive, and to do that we need to know what you think. Thus, we look forward to hearing more about how you made the exercises work for you. It is very rewarding as a teacher to hear that students remember and use the information, methods, and techniques they learned in classes that we taught. Such has been the case with these exercises. For example, we keep hearing from students who to this day are still adapting and using their introductions they created from "Representing Yourself Professionally as an Anthropologist: The Introduction Exercise."

Based on all of the above, you can see that we would very much appreciate hearing from you in the future. Please tell us what you did with these exercises and if any interesting insights or other things come of them. Please make suggestions for improvement. We are a community of anthropologists, and we welcome your contributions. We want to hear about your experiences so we can share them with others who will benefit from using these materials in the future. You may reach either of us through the contact information available on our university department's webpage at www.clas.wayne.edu/Anthropology/.

II

PROFESSIONAL
DEVELOPMENT EXERCISES

EXERCISE 1

Understanding Yourself as an Anthropologist

The Identity Expedition Exercise

Activity Overview

This first exercise is a fun self-exploration that will help you begin to understand yourself as an anthropologist. You can do this exercise on your own, or you can do it in a group setting such as a class or a party that you host for your friends. (If you are doing this activity in a group setting, consider setting a ten- or fifteen-minute time limit on each person's presentation so everyone is able to have a turn.) Either way, be creative, and have fun!

Instructions

Step 1

Gather things that represent the many facets of you. These things can be material objects, such as books, art, or pictures. These things can be what you have created—sketches drawn, collages assembled, or music written. These things can represent important relationships or sentiments—people you love, a song that inspires you, a poem that is meaningful, or a powerful scent. Don't feel limited by our suggestions—look around your home, your workplace, and the spaces where you spend the most time to find the things you have a powerful connection with. If the items are too fragile or too ephemeral to physically gather, take a picture or write a description you can share.

Step 2

Either on your own or with your group, explain what each thing you chose represents. What meaning does each thing have for you? Describe how the things relate to each other, which are the most valuable to you and why. What is motivating about these things? Think about what is anthropological about this assembly of things. How do they potentially fit in with your work life? What is the story that this collection of things tells about you?

Self-Reflection

Write a paragraph or two on the experience of doing this exercise. Describe your approach to the assignment—what does that tell you? Did you collect a few deeply meaningful things or have a broader range of objects? How easy or difficult was it to explain how the things related to one another? What insights did you gain about yourself from doing the exercise? Can you anticipate how your insights might change in a year, or in ten years?

Follow-Up Activities

- Host a party where everyone brings a collection of things that represent aspects of who they are and take turns excavating your identities.
- Find the insights that illustrate why you're an anthropologist!

Sample Exercise Completed by Anne, a Ph.D. Student

For this exercise, Anne hosted a party, as suggested in the Follow-Up Activities. She sent an email invitation to seven people from her circle of friends and colleagues (including us, the authors), offering dinner and requesting that everyone follow the instructions for the exercise for the evening's activity.

On the designated evening, all seven people participated in the exercise after a social dinner. Each person took a turn displaying and describing the items they brought to the event, the meaning the items had, and what was anthropological about their choices. Most people brought items with specific meanings, such as books, rings, pictures, sculptures, diaries, and toys. One participant created a picture slideshow set to music to display her "identity." Pictures from Anne's Identity Expedition party, showing her displaying and describing her objects and her written responses to the exercise, are given here. Comments in parentheses are by the authors, providing more context for the reader.

Photo by Amy Goldmacher.

Step 1

Objects:
- Picture of Mom
- Coffee pot with sign of Islam (purchased in the grand sooque in Damascus)
- Statue of Virgin Mary (wedding gift)
- Hanukkah Menorah (Christmas present from brother-in-law John)

Step 2

Anne's Identity and Choice of Objects I was raised in a devout Catholic family in Minnesota. My parents and other family members worked in healthcare. My father is a doctor and my mother is a nurse. The lives of my parents provided me with daily illustrations of the reciprocal relationship between belief and practice. I saw how their Catholic faith informed their work, and more importantly, I was able to see how their faith was always informed by the realities of their work. I have been most influenced by my mother whom I think is one of the finest creatures ever born. I chose to include a newspaper photo and article profiling her many

Photo by Amy Goldmacher.

years of work in adolescent healthcare. While she influenced me to become a nurse, she was the most surprised over my choice of this same profession. She knew I had many interests.

After college, I joined the U.S. Peace Corps and worked as a nurse volunteer in North Yemen. The coffee pot with the sign of Islam purchased in the grand sooque in Damascus represents this important period in my life and how my interest in health issues cross-culturally grew and developed. This major experience coupled with my professional practice as a home care nurse in diverse ethnic communities within metropolitan Detroit led me to later study anthropology. I became increasingly interested in the role of culture in human responses to illness and disease and went on to graduate studies within medical anthropology. I am especially intrigued by cross-cultural studies of emotion and mental health. My dissertation research focuses on health concerns of Arab immigrants and refugees, especially as they relate to mental health.

Following my Peace Corps experience in the Middle East, I returned to the United States and married a Jewish man. Despite the differences in our faith backgrounds, because religious tradition had played such central roles in both our families, we had a lot in common. This *assumption* of similarity made it easy for us to agree on a plan to raise any eventual children in the Jewish faith. It wasn't until the birth of our first child that I began to be pulled into and aware of the differences between our two worlds. It wasn't until I began to "practice," at the time, for my children, that I began to really become aware of the differences in thinking and views between our two faith traditions. When I began to study Judaism more formally, all the while incorporating more ritual celebration into my home, I began to become more curious about the relationship between structures, rituals, beliefs, and how one comes to order one's world. The statue of the Virgin Mary, given to us as a wedding gift by a well-meaning relative, remains out on display in our Jewish home because both my husband and I recognize it as a contribution to our family identity. These continual back and forth comparisons, no doubt extended to my work as a nurse. In assessing how my patients were dealing with their illnesses, more and more of my questions became focused on developing an understanding of where my patient came from, what they believed, and what they did. The awareness of and the interest in different perspectives and different life ways began with watching my parents adjust their thinking as the result of their contact with variety and difference.

Anne's Thoughts about Her Objects Displayed and Their Relationships to Her Identity   Each object represents a sphere of influence. They are presented in chronological order of experience. All spheres continue to influence, sometimes in ways that are familiar and sometimes in ways that are new, each adding to and changing the other. When I look at them I think of moments of departure and return. Always departure and always return.

In my life, I have traveled and I have crossed cultures many times, which has made me think deeply. Like an anthropologist, I think that whatever has led to my coming and my going, being within and then the eventual leaving is my way of finding "a good view," or "the best seat," in order to make sense of everything. I think the movement has a lot to do with the search for counterpoint. I think all anthropologists are looking for that great view.

The menorah is a confused object that is one of my most prized possessions. It is confused because the maker tried to reproduce a ritual object, or symbol, for a ritual he did not understand. As a result he put in cultural symbols that had meaning for him. The high value I place on this menorah has to do with its maker, my practical, optimistic, Swedish Presbyterian brother-in-law. He would say with a smile, "Why do what is meaningless?" I also know he was motivated out of a desire to please. [The menorah is a Jewish ritual object that holds lit candles during Hanukkah. This menorah, created by Anne's brother-in-law, is crafted out of wood, and the candle holders are wood painted Christmasy colors of red and gold. The menorah was used in the past, but some pieces had burned away.] Any full explanation of the meaning of this object must then contain more than the identification of cultural symbols and their origins; it must also attend to the relationship of the individual to culture. Without the subjectiveness of John, there would be no odd mix. The fact that I delight in the mix is a quality that I think anthropologists must have. We delight in odd mixes.

Anne's Self-Reflection after the Exercise   This was not a difficult exercise for me. It did have the effect of firming up my ideas and it was interesting to see others in the group making similar observations. . . . I think Andrea's [another participant at the party] observation that the presentations of younger group members seemed to be different from those of older group members hit on something, although I would like to think about it more. I have thought a lot about the different spheres I have moved between so far in my life . . . family of origin, Catholicism, Judaism, Arab culture, academia . . . probably because the shifting I do to accommodate myself to "sphere change" is not always comfortable or easy. Perhaps it is because the spheres are so distinct. Christianity and Judaism involve very different ways of ordering the world. My family of origin and academia are distinct . . . yet all these spheres have things in common. These spheres also overlap with my chronological life course experience. When I was a child I was submerged in a Catholic world. As a new parent I was heavily into a Jewish world . . . as a mature adult, I entered into the world of formal scholarship.

These larger spheres of influence stood out more for me, more than the details of what I like or what I do, more than who I am exactly, the roles I occupy, my hobbies. For example, in my explanation to the group, I believe I mentioned that I was a nurse, but not in my written statement. I might have brought up more of these "details" with a group who did not know me. "Being a nurse" seems to fit into the spheres of "family of origin," and Catholicism. I could look at my roles and activities as being part of the sphere at the time. Years from now I might look at these four spheres as having a lot more in common or as being a part of some larger more inclusive category. I would expect that my perspective would change with time.

EXERCISE 2

Understanding Your Educational Background

The Transcript Exercise

Activity Overview

This exercise will help you summarize your academic coursework and create concise descriptions about how your education is relevant to the job you are seeking. When you look at courses listed on a transcript, the course titles do not adequately describe what you have learned from the class. It is up to you to be able to convey to potential employers how and why the courses you took provided you with relevant and useful skills. Moving from the course title and the academic course description, you will describe how your education has prepared you for the job you are seeking.

Instructions

Step 1

Create a table of courses taken (as shown in Table II.2.1) to summarize your academic experiences.

Step 2

Describe your courses using short, jargon-free phrases, or take descriptions from your course syllabi, if appropriate. Succinctly explain how your coursework has given you relevant skills. List brief but memorable examples from class as vivid illustrations of why these skills are relevant in the workplace. Look at the "Toolkit of a Good Professional Anthropologist" provided in Part I to find useful language for describing what you learned from your class projects.

Step 3

Practice talking about how your academic coursework has prepared you for the job you are seeking. Talk to friends, classmates, your mentor, your advisor, or potential employers.

Table II.2.1. Sample Table of Courses

Course Title	Course Description	Relevant Skills	Memorable Class Example(s)
Applied Anthropology	Application of anthropological concepts and methods to contemporary issues of public concern	a. I learned about different jobs where you can apply knowledge from anthropology's subfields. b. I learned how to use various anthropological methods, such as participant observation and interviewing, to solve problems.	To help a client develop a new breakfast food, an anthropologist worked with a team of product designers to observe families' breakfast behaviors. They found that kids liked to eat foods that were fun and portable, and parents wanted their kids to eat nutritious foods. The findings helped the breakfast company develop "Go-GURT," which responded to the unmet needs of both kids and parents (Jordan 2003).
Discourse Analysis	Class focused on a method that can be used in conjunction with other qualitative data analysis methods to provide additional insights into speech and speaking	How people talk is just as important as what they are talking about. This method allows you to look deeper into the content of what people are saying and find culturally constructed ways of speaking that reveal much about the speakers.	Men and women tend to communicate in different ways. Research has found that women, in general, use rising intonations at the end of utterances to invite others to respond, but this technique is interpreted by men, in general, as sounding insecure and weak. These types of communication differences may result in miscommunication in meetings (Tannen 1994).

Self-Reflection

- In what ways can you use what you learned from this exercise in your career planning? Do you see how you can rearrange the courses presented in Table II.2.1 up or down according to how relevant they are to the job you are applying for and to help you focus on the most pertinent topics? Write one or two paragraphs about why understanding your educational background using this framework could help you in landing a job and developing your career over time.

Follow-Up Activities

- Use the material from Table II.2.1 to develop a set of talking points, so you can practice saying aloud precisely how each class gave you a specific skill, as though you were in a job interview. Consider how you could use the memorable examples from these classes to communicate to a potential employer the "value-added" of anthropology for a particular job situation.
- Write a cover letter as if you were submitting your own resumé and transcript to this potential employer. As you write, consult your table to help you highlight how your skills gained through coursework are relevant to the job you are applying for.

Sample Exercise Completed by Jennifer, an MA Student

Steps 1 and 2 (see Table II.2.2 on the next page, which is the student's model)

Jennifer's Self-Reflection   The process of compiling this chart has helped me to organize and remember various things I have learned and accomplished in my educational career. Many of the memorable experiences are related to research that was done for each class. After reviewing the memorable experiences from each class, the qualities that I find enjoyable become more apparent. This information can help me to look for job positions that relate to such experiences. When applying for research jobs in the future, this chart will aid in preparing for interviews and writing cover letters that have specific examples of the skills I have obtained from my education. In the event that I was applying for a different type of job (i.e., nonresearch), I could use the information from the other columns to create new memorable experiences that relate to the job in which I am applying.

Understanding how coursework fits within personal career development is important because often there are specific qualities that are wanted for specific job opportunities. This exercise is an essential tool to prepare for future interviews and have specific answers to questions that may arise during the interview. The tool not only is a way to remember certain concepts that were discussed in the past but also to have documented experiences in an organized chart that have been enjoyable throughout the educational portion of my career building.

Table II.2.2. Sample Courses Offered in the Field of Anthropology

Course Title	Course Description*	Relevant Skills	Memorable Class Experience
ANT: Introduction to Anthropology	Study of humanity, past and present: cultural diversity and change, human evolution, biological variability, archaeology, ethnography, language, and contemporary uses of anthropology.	1. Basic understanding of the four fields of anthropology.	Discussion on the cultural construction of race. Field interview regarding race with a WSU student.
ANT: Biology and Culture	Interrelationships between the cultural and biological aspects of humans; human genetic variability, human physiological plasticity and culture as associated mechanisms by which humans adapt to environmental stress.	1. Learning how biology and culture work synergistically together. 2. Basic understanding of physical anthropology.	Writing an annotated bibliography for research paper.
ANT: Applied Anthropology	The application of anthropological concepts and methods to contemporary issues of public concern in the United States and abroad.	1. Determining jobs that are available for applied anthropologists. 2. Understanding how anthropology is useful in many applied situations.	Interviewing an epidemiologist about her job position and determining how an anthropologist would be well suited for similar job positions.
ANT: Research Methods	Intensive introduction to research methods, techniques and issues in anthropology. Students engage in a research experience supervised by the instructor, write a field journal, and complete a final exam. Exercises focus on data collection, data management,	1. ATLAS.ti* Knowledge 2. Creating contacts in the community. 3. Learning the major steps to fieldwork. 4. Research techniques.	Conducting my first ethnography—interviewing, participant observation, analysis using ATLAS.ti* and writing a report on the findings.

	and data analysis. Techniques include participant observation, field notes, and interviewing. Students learn how to use software packages employed by anthropological researchers in the computer lab.		
ANT: Language Societies	Contemporary linguistic anthropologists see language as a form of social action. How has this understanding of language in society evolved? Read classic works of linguistic anthropology and contemporary studies in this growing field. Engage in research on language in society.	1. Basic understanding of linguistic anthropology. 2. Learning about the cultural construction of the way people speak.	Conducting field research on healthcare and patient interactions by comparing presentation styles of healthcare professionals in various situations.
ANT: Health and Illness	Concepts and theory in medical anthropology from cultural and biological perspectives. Topics include: cross-cultural aspects of sex and gender in health and illness, life course, sexuality, birth and death, bio-cultural approaches to healing and treatment, international health and epidemiology.	1. Learning the different approaches used in medical anthropology. 2. Applying medical anthropology approaches to healthcare issues.	Reading Lynn Payer's book *Medicine and Culture* and discussing the differences in medical systems depending on context.

(continued)

Table II.2.2. *(continued)*

Course Title	Course Description*	Relevant Skills	Memorable Class Experience
ANT: Community Health Ethnography	Field placement in a health service agency. Students provide volunteer assistance to an agency while conducting participant observation research exercises. Utilization of field experience to earn about urban health issues and research methodology.	1. Participant observation. 2. Interviewing skills. 3. Interpretation of data. 4. Incorporating theory into applied work.	Presenting the findings of participant observation and interviews to project staff at the location of my internship and receiving excellent reviews from the organization.
ANT: Gender, Sex, Sexuality	We will explore a number of topics, including: the biological realities of human sexual differentiation, the cultural construction and constantly shifting dimensions of gender and sexuality; the impact of colonialism and economic development in shaping constructions of gender and sexuality; "the holy trinity" of class, race and gender and its intersection with legalized moralities; and the ways in which gender and sexuality shape contemporary U.S. culture and society.	1. Learning about relevant arguments in regards to gender, sex, and sexuality. 2. Class discussion on topics.	Discussion on the history of sex and sexuality in America and how the history helps to shape views of gender at present.
ANT: Medical Anthropology Theory I	Core concepts and theoretical approaches, including: aging, life course, childhood, old age, disability, chronic illness,	1. Studying theoretical and philosophical arguments in regards to medical anthropology.	Trying to understand Foucault, Latour, Kristeva, and other philosophers and incorporating the authors and ideas into theoretically informed papers.

infectious disease, international health, organization of health care institutions, health policy, political economy of health, women's health, reproduction, technology; the body, bioethics, culture and cognition, death and dying, race and ethnicity, violence, sex and sexuality.

2. Relating other disciplines to medical anthropology.

1. Applying theoretical arguments to ethnographic fieldwork

2. Learning how to write a book review

3. Academic professionalization skills

Obtaining IRB approval and completion of an ethnographic field project with a theoretical component. This paper may be published in the future.

*The course descriptions were obtained from either the course syllabi or WSU course description.

EXERCISE 3

Understanding Your Work Background

The Job Titles Exercise

Activity Overview

Nowadays most anthropology graduates will not hold positions with the job title of anthropologist. This exercise is designed to help you think about how you will still be working as an anthropologist, regardless of what you are called! To develop this mindset, you will consider the work that you have done before and analyze how it was anthropological. Gaining this perspective on your prior work will help you with moving forward in planning your anthropologically oriented career.

Instructions

Step 1

List the titles of all jobs that you have held. This list is not restricted to paid employment, so you can list volunteer jobs, being a stay-at-home parent, being a caregiver to a family member, or teaching a friend how to do something.

Step 2

For each job on your list, write a couple of sentences or a short paragraph discussing the nature of this work. Create a table like Table II.3.1 to help you organize your experiences. Keeping in mind the broad definition of anthropology as a field covering many different aspects of the human experience, what could be seen as anthropological about each job? What were the formal and informal activities associated with this job? What skills are related to the subfields? How did each job influence your career path to date? To assist you in writing your descriptions, we recommend you have "The Toolkit of a Good Professional Anthropologist" from Part I in front of you to help you find the anthropological language to explain your experiences and the skills you gained.

Table II.3.1. Sample of Job Experiences List

Job Title	How Was It Anthropological?	What Did You Take Away from This Experience That Informs Your Career Development?
Newspaper Delivery Person	Regularly delivered newspapers to various neighborhoods; observed differences in houses and types of papers people read; experienced range of tipping behaviors	Learned about socioeconomic status and cultural practices regarding tipping behavior
Fast Food Employee	Interacted with coworkers and customers; observed how people act with food; saw how organization tries to standardize operations and product delivery through training	Learned how to get along with many kinds of people; saw how food is a very integral part of social networks and culture; learned about how individuals adapt corporate practices in local environment
Doggie Daycare Worker	Observed relationships of humans and other species; learned about notions of kinship among dog owners through conversations about pet ownership and how pets are classified as family members; experienced rite of passage when promoted from daycare worker to daycare supervisor	Learned about human/animal interaction; learned about of cultural practices relating to dog care, including ritual and symbolic aspects; participated in an organizational and hierarchical work culture
Martial Arts Instructor	Taught the cultural and historical background and philosophy of the discipline; explained material culture (e.g., symbolism of garments worn and tools used); managed groups of people of varying abilities; created and taught material	Enjoyed learning about and sharing cultural aspects of this sport; liked leading people and being a positive influence; liked doing participant observation and seeing how this sport is practiced in different settings
College Textbook Sales Representative	Interviewed professors to understand their textbook needs and reported back to company; observed inter- and intragroup variation on campuses; traveled to various locations	Liked collecting information to provide solutions; enjoyed developing relationships with customers; liked travel

Self-Reflection

Write one or two paragraphs reflecting on the experience of doing this exercise. Discuss what you have discovered about how your work history to date has been an anthropological one. Envision ways you can now build on this list as you continue to develop your anthropological career.

Follow-Up Activities

- Practice using your anthropological mindset by reviewing a series of want ads in your local paper or online. What could be anthropological about each of these job postings?
- Take the job list you created in this exercise and compare it to your current resumé, if you have one. If not, you can take the opportunity now to make a draft of a formal resumé (which can also be used in the "Resume Exercise" later on). Could you add any of your informal experience to your professional resumé to flesh it out? Can you create a fuller story of your experience and highlight how your background is an anthropological one?

Sample Exercise Completed by Angela, an MA Student

For this exercise, Angela wrote about jobs she had, describing each with an anthropological perspective in a narrative format instead of using a table.

Step 1

Animal Shelter Assistant—This was a great opportunity to begin honing my participant observation skills. While I provided basic care for the animals I learned about the culture of a Humane Society and how humane treatment of animals was viewed in a farming community in Iowa. In this town, animals were viewed as workers, income, and food. Most people didn't see the need for an animal rescue. When an animal was old or sick someone would shoot it.

Paper Delivery Person—There are only two anthropological experiences that I can associate with delivering the paper. The first experience that delivering the paper provided me with was mapping the neighborhoods in my small Iowa college town. The farther I delivered from the college, the fewer people subscribed to the paper. The second anthropological experience that delivering the paper provided me was as sort of a foreign observer. We were the only black family in town and my paper route brought me in contact with a lot of people who were curious about me. When we moved to this town, everyone knew who we were and that my father was a professor. I can only imagine that an anthropologist in the field might have similar experiences.

Waitress at the College Club—Another great opportunity to hone participant observation skills. I got to view the hierarchy at the club and on campus.

Girl Scout Camp Counselor—I worked at a Girl Scout Camp the summer after my sophomore year in high school. We lived in a small northeastern Louisiana town that was home to two state universities. The camp was located about fifteen miles west of the town. Again, I was a participant observer, and I had the opportunity to see Southern race relations up close and personal.

My father taught at the historically black university (HBU), and my sister and I attended the HBU's laboratory high school. There were no white kids at our school. The campers came from all over the northern part of the state and were about 60 percent white and 40 percent black. I learned that the cabins were segregated by race even though the director said the cabins were divided by troop. The counselors' cabin was integrated. It was my first blatant view at how organizations reinforce segregation.

Camp Counselor at Chicago Youth Centers Camp—This job brought me to Eau Claire, Michigan, which is about five miles outside of St. Joseph/Benton Harbor area, a pair of communities known to be highly segregated between blacks and whites. This camp was huge: about 500 campers and 50 full-time counselors. The campers and the counselors were ethnically diverse. Some of the counselors were from the UK. My anthropological experience at this summer job was to observe how a diverse group of people are treated in a racially hostile environment. When we took the kids bike riding to the dunes, townspeople from St. Joe would yell "take the niggers back to Benton Harbor."

Babysitter—Great opportunity to observe the cultural norms of the "townies" in Wellesley, Massachusetts. Being a student at the college, babysitting was my only opportunity to interact with the town's people. The jobs were passed down from student to student through referral. The pay was great.

Research Assistant for the Detroit Area Study—This job provided me with my first opportunity to interview people. This was also my first "real" research job.

General Assistant at a Techno Record Label—I received firsthand experience about the culture of the music business and working in a male-dominated industry. Again, I was honing my participant observation skills.

Graduate Research Assistant in College of Urban, Labor and Metropolitan Affairs—My first job as a graduate student. I was a program evaluator for community health groups receiving City of Detroit funding. I used my participant observation skills, interviewing skills, and learned how to evaluate a program and write a report of my findings.

Graduate Research Assistant for the Dean of College of Urban, Labor and Metropolitan Affairs—I learned a lot about the culture of the academy and observed how the academic hierarchy works. I interviewed people and organized a conference. Great job to be a participant observer who is interested in issues of gender and race in the academy.

Graduate Research Assistant for Medical Anthropologist—I learned a lot about qualitative data analysis. I also learned the importance of a sound conceptual framework for any research project. Great opportunity to watch an anthropologist in action.

Angela's Self-Reflection   I thought the assignment was very beneficial because I began to see how my current research interests were formed. Of course I realize that I didn't know that I would be interested in issues of race/class/gender when I was a kid working at the Humane Society in Iowa. However, this assignment allowed me to reflect about what I thought was meaningful in all of my work experience; through my reflection I know that issues of race/class/gender fascinate me.

EXERCISE 4

Understanding Your Values

The Code of Ethics Exercise

Activity Overview

Because anthropologists have such diverse responsibilities, it is especially important to consider the influence of your personal code of ethics on your work life. For example, at the time of this writing, a big debate exists among anthropologists as to their role in military operations and whether they should be involved at all. Many aspects of your personal history will shape your values, expectations, and social interactions. In this exercise, you will have the chance to consider how aspects of your personal, cultural, educational, and work background contribute to your own code of ethics. You can then consider the relationship of your personal code of ethics to your anthropological career.

Instructions

Step 1

The following five prompts will help you start thinking about your core beliefs (The authors credit Bill Braun for his original work, *The Personal Mastery Project*, from which this exercise was adapted for anthropologists.) Choose at least two that inspire you and write at least a one-paragraph response. Some people initially find making a definitive statement about their beliefs challenging; a good way to start may be to think of the things you know you absolutely won't do, or what lines you won't cross. You could write these out, type them out, or create a collage of images—choose a method that will help you organize your thoughts.

- These things are true for me:

- I value most:

- These influences guide my personal and professional decisions:

- These are my core beliefs:

- They come from:

Look at what you came up with. Does it surprise you in any way? Why or why not? Do you feel that you mostly live by these principles now? What gets in your way of doing so?

Step 2

Now it's time to think about how your anthropology education relates to your core beliefs and values. Reflect on some key ideas from your anthropology coursework to address the prompts. You could pull out books or notes from your courses to help you formulate your answers. Choose at least two and write a paragraph or more in response. Feel free to choose to respond to all the prompts for the most self-reflection and material to work with when you reach Step 3.

- What does it mean to be human?

- How does anthropology contribute to a greater appreciation for a diversity of people and ways of thinking?

- What does it mean to think holistically and comparatively in anthropology?

- What does it mean to *you* to work ethically as an anthropologist?

Step 3

Drawing from what you've articulated, now write out your personal code of ethics. It can be as brief as one paragraph or it might be considerably longer. Just make sure that you feel it captures the essence of your core beliefs and your anthropological perspective.

Self-Reflection

Write one or two paragraphs reflecting on the experience of doing this exercise. Discuss what you have discovered about your own ethical stance, how your anthropology education has contributed to developing that stance, and how you will make use of this knowledge in the future. Talk about the relevance of your code of ethics for both your personal and professional lives.

Follow-Up Activities

- Read the American Anthropological Association's (AAA) statement of ethics and compare/contrast it to your personal code of ethics.
- Read about historic ethical debates in anthropology. Find relevant sources in the library, on the Internet (e.g., AAA website), and by asking your mentors where to look.

Sample Exercise Completed by Jasmine, an Undergraduate Student

---

Step 1

These things are true for me: I am interpreting this concept of "true for me" as what I believe is often the case from my experiences in life and what I believe are patterns to our human existence. Authority figures do not always make decisions and/or behave in the best interest of others. The formative years in children's lives are very important in shaping them as adults. Inequality of education, resources, and opportunities lead to class and status differences and vice versa, that force some to struggle more than others with fulfilling their basic needs in the United States. I believe that conflicts can be resolved without resorting to war and violence. I believe that prejudice and racism often stem from lack of exposure, ignorance, and family legacy. I believe that it is wrong and unfair that one must have a large amount of money or a rarely found job that offers insurance in order to have health care in this country. I believe that if you talk to someone long enough no matter how different you and that person may be, you can find something in common. I believe that we humans have the responsibility to care for our environment just as much as we have the power to alter it.

I value most: Equality, respect, learning, honesty, emotional sensitivity, patience, courage to overcome obstacles, persistence, cooperation, peace, environmentalism, and advocacy.

These influences guide my personal and professional decisions: I feel that my childhood experiences have affected the choices I've made regarding my personal life and professional goals. I grew up in a household with a Chinese-Thai and Buddhist mother and a mixed European and Baptist father. I also had Yemeni, Indian, and Filipino neighbors, and was friends with practicing Catholics, Baptists, Muslims, and Jehovah's Witnesses. My neighborhood was a bit more diverse than most people assume Taylor, Michigan, would be. These interactions with my friends and neighbors and my own personal struggle with identity have influenced my interests in learning about various cultures and how detrimental prejudice and racism are to our communities. I have realized that studying anthropology sheds much light on the misconceptions people have about others due to their ignorance and lack of exposure. I feel that it is important for children to learn about diversity and differences, and that cooperation with others is a useful method to learn, interact, and work with those whom they might otherwise have avoided. I also struggled throughout my childhood with an alcoholic parent and received little emotional and mental support from either one of my two parents. I have struggled with self-esteem, but have persisted to overcome financial, mental, and emotional obstacles with self-motivation.

I spent much of my time working many different jobs, mostly in the service industry, in order to get by on my own. This along with social interests was why I didn't finish school so quickly. I also was unsure about what to study in college. After I took a world religions course and finally met an anthropologist I realized that this is the field that I wanted to learn more about. A Pell grant, some scholarships, and a big loan later, I was back in school and more focused than ever in the past. I have realized over the years how important children's experiences and education are to creating our future adults. These experiences along with my brief stint as an ice cream truck driver inspired me to combine my interests in anthropology and children's education. I began to consider a double major for a bachelor's degree in anthropology as well as elementary education, but surprisingly I found that anthropology is not recognized as a major within the education program at our university since it is not considered subject matter for primary or secondary school education. I then became interested in education policies such as "No Child Left Behind" and classroom language policies (bilingual versus monolingual instruction for immigrant students), which sometimes seem to maintain inequality in communities.

I feel that my experiences as a child taught me the importance of supporting and protecting those who are without power and those who are underprivileged because they often don't have a voice that can be heard. These ideas are related to my interests in education and public policy now. My sentiments about these topics extend to people, other species, and the environment.

These are my core beliefs: I believe that all life is interconnected and that nothing occurs in isolation. We as humans (on individual and international levels as well) not only affect each other's lives and ideas, but also the environment and other species. I also believe strongly in karma and reincarnation; that all we do will return to us at some point in the future, whether it's in this life or another.

They come from: I feel that my belief in interconnectedness stems from some of my difficult experiences in which another's behavior or words affected me. Seeing how someone else's insensitivities can harm another has made me more aware and conscious of my own behavior toward others. It has motivated me to consider my own actions and how they may affect others. I also feel that perhaps my belief in karma stems from a desire to see some type of justice in the world that cannot be swayed by money or who one knows; a faceless force that gives returns for one's past actions, and provides people with opportunities to learn and grow from their mistakes by making them experience the receiving end of their actions.

What surprises me about what I've written during this exercise is where my belief in karma may come from. I think that it validates my value in learning and education. There is some comfort for me to believe that somehow people can learn through experience and change behaviors that cause suffering in others, but at the same time I don't feel that karma alone will change the injustice and suffering in the world. One must act in order to create positive change.

I feel that I do live by many of the principles I've discussed previously, but I feel that I'm not where I'd like to be in terms of my career path. I think that what is getting in the way of accomplishing this is that I just received my bachelor's degree and must return to grad school. I need to continue my education in order to learn more about my research interests and which topics have been addressed within the field of anthropology of education. Another obstacle is that I spend much of my time working as a waitress, catering bartender, and part-time caretaker in order to cover my living expenses with a flexible schedule necessary for class enrollment.

Step 2

What does it mean to be human? The human experience entails the ability to creatively communicate with others through the use of symbols. These symbols include gestures and spoken languages that are taught and learned through social interaction. Culture is another unique characteristic of the human experience that varies worldwide. It is the sets of learned behaviors, norms, and beliefs systems that we often embrace as the normal and appropriate way to exist in the world. We humans use our language as a tool to inquire why and how in order to create some understanding about ourselves and our environment. Humans have created multitudes of explanations that often give us comfort or some type of control over ourselves and our surroundings. Humans also have a unique ability to create a wide variety of tools for enhancing communication and altering the environment. I feel that along with this human power to shape our environment comes a responsibility to consider its impact on other species.

How does anthropology contribute to a greater appreciation for a diversity of people and ways of thinking? Anthropology has the ability to reveal the multiple variations of how people experience and view the world. It exposes the fact that there isn't just one way to experience life and that all of our behaviors are learned and passed on by those who raise us and surround us throughout our lives. I have realized throughout my anthropological education that perhaps there isn't a correct or wrong way to live; it really is a matter of what is taught as acceptable and normal in your current location. There is also a struggle to balance the concepts of human rights versus cultural relativism. There are certain behaviors and beliefs that harm others and are not always accepted by anthropologists as simply culturally relevant. I have learned to avoid ethnocentrism through my anthropological studies so that I can have the ability to attempt to understand other cultures and behaviors without simply dismissing them as wrong or illogical. Condemning a behavior or belief does not develop understanding, but often hinders it. Anthropology has taught me that since there are such a wide variety of ways to live, I actually have a choice in how I would like to view and experience the world.

What does it mean to think holistically and comparatively in anthropology? To think holistically is to consider all parts of a system as connected and influential to each other. It is looking at many different aspects of a culture, an institution, a situation, a personal experience, and so forth and seeing that nothing is isolated. Religious systems, economic systems, social systems, and governing systems are tied together and affect each other. The present and future are connected and influenced by the past interactions and events. Ideas are a culmination of what has been learned from the past and added to in the present.

Comparative thought is important in anthropology. In order to compare several cultures, one must balance emic and etic perspectives. This balance allows us to take several emic perspectives and find common threads or concepts. Our own "etic terms" are used to describe different behaviors, beliefs, values, and systems and apply it to the various cultural texts that we are analyzing. These etic terms make discussion and cross-cultural analysis possible for anthropologists.

What does it mean to me to work ethically as an anthropologist? It is important to me that I work ethically as an anthropologist. It means having control over my research findings and information and knowing that it will not be used to harm or take advantage of others. I feel very skeptical about working for a government or military agency since I would lose control over how my data could be used. I have read of past anthropologists whose work was used to undermine and disadvantage Native American groups and others especially during hostile and war times. I am interested in public education and wonder if I would have to be employed by some aspect of a government agency. I would prefer to have my future research supported by a university instead. I feel that working ethically means that no harm will be done to those who are involved in the fieldwork or research study. It means protecting their identity if they so wish and making every effort not to misrepresent what I have learned or discovered through research and fieldwork. It is very important to capture as much as possible, the insider emic perspective by being honest with the consultants I am working with. Often anthropologists doing fieldwork attempt to be conscious about their presence and how it may alter the culture or society that they are working with. Since I am interested in some level of advocacy work within the education system here in the United States, I feel that my stance may be somewhat different. I feel that I would have to be "objective" in the process of gathering information, but in the future I would like the research data to be used to improve the quality of life and education for young students in the public education system.

My own personal code of ethics: I feel that my actions should be guided by the desire to reduce suffering and help create equality and protection among humans and other species. I will be conscious of how my career and behavior affects others. My actions should help enhance understanding and cooperation without force or destruction. I will respect others' opinions and worldviews by listening and interacting. I will always oppose stereotypes with counterexamples. I will remember that suspending judgment and condoning an action are two different things. I will suspend judgment until I am able to understand why the event or action is happening, then I will decide whether I agree with it or not.

Jasmine's Self-Reflection   This exercise has been insightful for me in many ways. It has allowed me to look more closely at my own values and beliefs and see how they may have formed and how they shape my career goals as an anthropologist. I feel that my ethical stance to respect others, improve conditions, protect those who do not have a strong voice stems from my own personal experiences of feeling powerless, unprotected, and disadvantaged. I would like to use this drive and motivation toward improving the lives and opportunities of others. I think that childhood development is very important in creating our future adults who will later make decisions that impact our societies and policies. I feel that respecting one another's opinions and values plays a crucial role in self-development and self-esteem, for without self-esteem, motivation, and hope one may not reach his or her full potential. Anthropology has taught me the importance of cultural relativity and how this concept allows one to gain a clearer understanding that different humans see the life experience through multiple lenses and that one is not particularly better than another. This reinforced my ethical stance of respecting others. The strict AAA guidelines of fieldwork and research also supported my established view that I should avoid causing harm and suffering of others.

I feel that my code of ethics is very relevant to my professional life choices. My future plans to do research in the field of education is motivated by the desire to create equality in terms of educational opportunities for young students in the public school system. Some of this involves researching and understanding policies that involve standardized testing. The new policies require that high scores be achieved in order to gain additional funding and resources for the school districts. Therefore, those schools that have poor test scores are often short on resources and impoverished and do not receive the financial support and improvements that are needed. I am also interested in learning more about language policies in the classroom and how they affect recent immigrant students. I feel that my career goals to do this type of research are also motivated by other aspects of my code of ethics that involve enhancing understanding, cooperation, respect, and being conscious of how one's actions and policies affect others.

My personal life is also affected by these codes as well. I try to respect other species and the planet by contributing to organizations that help preserve wildlife and wildlife habitats. I also try to live and work in the same vicinity to avoid adding to our current pollution problem. I also live by the trio "reduce, reuse, and recycle." When I interact with others I try to suspend judgment and respect others' opinions in order to understand other points of view. I often argue against stereotypes with counterexamples in a respectful manner when conversations steer in that direction. I feel that the most challenging obstacle I have to overcome in terms of my personal code of ethics involves learning to be tolerant of intolerance. Others often have a drastically different view of diversity and express it openly. While I may embrace this diversity and feel curious to learn more about the various cultures and subcultures, many others reject it and condemn it without question.

This exercise has assisted me in revealing my values, where they come from, and how they affect my personal and professional choices. I am also reminded that personal experience changes the way we view the world and how we live. I also know that my personal and professional code of ethics will eventually shift somewhat in the not-so-distant future.

EXERCISE 5

Understanding Your Impact

The Social Change Exercise

Activity Overview

Now that you have written your own code of ethics, you can develop a strategy for addressing issues that you feel passionate about. You may be interested in working for social change either in your professional life, your personal life, or both. This exercise will help you think about how you can use your anthropological background and skill set to form an action plan to bring about social change on the issues that are most important to you.

Instructions

Step 1

Define the concepts below in your own way and think about their roles in your life. If you are having difficulties getting started, you can look up definitions for each of these terms in the dictionary or on the Internet and then modify these definitions to suit your own purposes. Try to get specific: is one term something you do and the other an outcome? How do you know it when you see it? Reflect on and respond to how you define these concepts and how they fit in your professional life, your personal life, or both.

- Activism is:

- Activism means to me:

- Social justice is:

- Social justice means to me:

Step 2

Identify several issues that are highly meaningful to you and are causes that you feel need to be addressed. For example, you could start by brainstorming a list of "-isms" (for example, racisim, sexism, ageism, classism) and decide which are most important for you to work on for creating a better society. Please note you do not need to confine yourself to "-isms" but can use other kinds of terms and topics as well, such as poverty, disability, environmental issues, and so forth.

Once you have chosen the issues that are most important to you, describe what role working on these issues currently plays in your life and to what extent you are satisfied with that level of involvement. How would you like that level of involvement to (potentially) change over time? Do you need additional experience or training to work effectively in this area? How can your anthropological background contribute to your success? Do you have connections, either personal or professional, who can help you?

Step 3

Make an action plan for your future involvement in working on these issues. You could create a timeline that shows the activities you will do over the next few years. You could list your desired roles and your expectations with tentative deadlines. How will you recognize success? What are some of the big and small indicators that you would want or expect to see? An example could be new legislation or more public awareness regarding your issues. Create something that will help you achieve your goals and identify improvements.

Self-Reflection

Write one to two paragraphs reflecting on the experience of doing this exercise. How do you see yourself working on these issues at different points in your life? What might motivate you to work harder on these issues or switch to a new area? How can your anthropological background enhance working well on these issues and bringing about social change over time?

Follow-Up Activities

- Write a letter to an agency, congressperson, or newspaper regarding one of the issues you identified as one way to take action. Use your anthropological mindset to frame your position (rather than writing a rant!).
- Develop an outreach strategy for getting others involved with your issue. For example, you could arrange to visit a grade school classroom to talk about environmental issues or give an informative talk to a seniors' group on how to develop an intergenerational mentorship program. Again, think about the ways in which your anthropological training could be helpful in developing your outreach strategy.

> ### *Sample Exercise Completed by Elena, an Undergraduate Student*

Step 1

What I did was look on the Internet at some different definitions to see their language used. I looked at dictionary.com, Wikipedia, and at other links that came up when I Googled "activism" and "social justice."

Then, I referred to the ideas in my personal code of ethics from Exercise 4: The Code of Ethics Exercise: courage, intellectual responsibility, respect for others, objectivity, integrity, honesty, confidentiality and loyalty, social responsibility, activism or advocacy, and appreciation for life and nature.

Activism is the practice of frequent action or involvement driven by some social, economic, or political orientation to possibly attain or influence a certain goal or purpose. Activism means to me that you are willing to stand up for your beliefs, your professional and personal code of ethics, put simplistically.

Social justice is a term used to describe the existence of fair and equal treatment in a society. Social justice means to me provision of the most basic human needs and rights to all individuals.

Step 2

While there are many issues important to me at this stage in my life, the three most important topics that mean the most to me are the following:

1. Provision of effective medical care
2. Violations of human rights
3. Environmental awareness

These issues matter to me most of all because they affect every single individual on this planet. Every individual needs effective medical care and our society still has a long road toward achieving that. More or less, every country violates human rights, I want to be able to at some point in my life contribute to prevention of those violations. Lastly, environmental awareness is something close to my heart because it allows for our very existence. I hope that someday I can have a part in promoting and sustaining a cleaner and more respected environment.

Even if some areas of these issues will require me to attain high training, having an anthropological background will be a great start as it provides me with a multifaceted inclination toward understanding. Additionally, my anthropology professors will most likely have something to offer in addition to my education (either in contacts or in guidance toward an approach).

Step 3

I believe it is not as important where you have been as where you are going. I am proud of my experiences, my hard work, and my education, and now I want to take it a step further. I hope that in the next few years I can:

1. Grow as an intellectual being.
2. Do more medically related research (hospital, clinics, or laboratories), to hopefully provide some insightful and critical knowledge to the medical arena.
3. Be actively involved in whatever it may be: writing in journals, reviews, publications, influencing public policy/legislation, community involvement, attending medical and science conferences, being part of medically affiliated organizations, all for promoting awareness and change.
4. Become a medical doctor in hopes of providing medical care in the country, or outside, to those in need; make an impact in local community or globally whether it is by writing a book, creating a medium of interaction between people, becoming actively involved in public policy or helping to improve conditions in areas where medical care may be desperately needed.
5. To constantly be active in knowing, being aware, and motivating others to know the importance of nature and environment as well as how that impacts the rest of our lives.

Elena's Self-Reflection This exercise has placed my beliefs, my goals, and my hope of success into perspective. I wish to achieve quite a lot; it will take time, and will probably occur progressively over the next five to ten years, as a start. These are the general scheme of things I wish, at the moment, to hopefully achieve for the future. The details may vary. Depending on the urgency or importance of the circumstance, I will be motivated to work harder, become more involved, or attain a new area of interest as it may require for intellectual growth, both personally and medically.

My anthropological education has provided me with a holistic approach to life, and most of all this will be key to enhancing my work on the issues above. Respect and appreciation for all individuals and cultures will help me achieve a more anthropological perspective in viewing any situation. Additionally, the following skills will also facilitate my growth and success: critical thinking and writing, obtaining detailed observations of an environment, good recordkeeping, the ability to draw patterns and reach conclusions from the gathered data.

EXERCISE 6

Understanding Yourself in Group Work

The Collaboration Exercise

Activity Overview

Anthropologists frequently work in group situations these days. They may work together with other anthropologists and/or those from other fields. In addition, working collaboratively may mean working with others in the same location, or it may mean working virtually with others who are not geographically located with you. This exercise will help you think about collaborative work, your own work style, and your role as an effective team member so that you can identify your strengths and weaknesses to potential employers.

Instructions

Step 1

Write a couple of sentences answering each of the following questions:

1. In your opinion, what are the pros of working in a group (e.g., different expertise, more perspectives, sharing knowledge, building consensus, learning opportunities, collective problem solving)?

2. What are the cons of working in a group (e.g., less autonomy and individual control, possibly more time-consuming, need for ongoing negotiations with team members)?

3. With these pros and cons in mind listed above in mind, what are some advantages and disadvantages for anthropologists generally and yourself specifically working in groups?

Step 2

Use Table II.6.1 on the next page to help you answer the following questions about a collaborative project you were involved in. This could be a class project, a work assignment, or an experience from volunteering. (If you get inspired, you can repeat this step considering other group projects in which you had a role.)

In the first column briefly *summarize the project*: describe its purpose, timeline, who was involved, and how group members communicated. For example, did you mainly work face to face, or did you regularly use communication technologies, such as email, the Internet, or phones?

In the second column, *explain your role in the group*. You could use terms such as leader, "worker bee," organizer, innovator, researcher, detail-oriented person, notekeeper, task manager, time manager, perfectionist, slacker, peacekeeper, person who pulled the final project together, proofreader, presenter, or some descriptive terms of your own to portray your role. Why did your role turn out that way? How would others describe your role? If there are differences in how you would describe your role from how others would describe it, what accounts for these differences?

In the third column, *write down some things you learned from working collaboratively with others on this group project*. What are the specific skills you gained from working collaboratively (e.g., learned about different ways of approaching/managing a project, gained knowledge of how to build consensus, used new collaboration software, etc.)?

In the fourth column, *consider what you would keep the same or change in your next group project*. In hindsight, what would you do differently to improve or build on this group work experience?

Table II.6.1.   Evaluating Your Role in Collaborative Work

Project Description	My Role	Key Insights	Suggestions for Future Group Work

Self-Reflection

Based on the assessment above, what have you learned about your experiences with group work? Knowing these things, what steps could you take to increase your comfort level when you enter into collaborative working situations and to better communicate with others? How does this knowledge impact the kinds of jobs you may look for now? How would you describe the "value added" of your anthropological skill-set for working collaboratively? Write a short statement based on what you learned from this exercise, or add another column to your table about how you view doing group work in your career going forward.

Follow-Up Activities

- Picture that you are at a job interview and are asked a specific question about your ability to work in groups. Imagine that you are also asked to provide an example of a time when you effectively did so. Use your notes from doing the exercise to create a concise and cogent answer. Practice your answer and get feedback if possible, both from those who have worked with you in groups as well as others.
- Write down several questions that you would like to ask your mentor(s) regarding their experiences with collaborative work. Share the table you have filled out in this exercise with them and receive feedback.
- Do some participant observation at your workplace or a volunteer organization. Ask to sit in on a project meeting for a group you are not involved in. Watch the dynamics closely and think about how the people are interacting and what is involved in creating that kind of interaction. (For this purpose, you are interested in studying how the group works collaboratively more closely than the activity they are engaged in.) Go through the questions above and analyze in the same way that you did previously for your own group project. Consider how it is different to make these observations as an outsider versus insider in the group.

Sample Exercise Completed by Terri Ann, a Ph.D. Student

Step 1

In your opinion, what are the pros of working in a group (e.g., different expertise, more perspectives, sharing knowledge, building consensus, learning opportunities, collective problem solving)? Building on a popular cliché, "Two heads are better than one," working in a group is valuable in that it allows for the wedding of different perspectives, the blending of multiple domains of expertise, and facilitates each member gaining new knowledge. Group work also advances the collaborative effort through the division of labor, with members often volunteering to handle specific tasks. When approached with an open mind, group work offers a unique arena, one that simultaneously promotes individual abilities and a collective learning experience.

What are the cons of working in a group (e.g., less autonomy and individual control, possibly more time-consuming, need for ongoing negotiations with team members)? A major detriment of working in a group is that all members must give up "control." While group work lends itself to advancing the individual members' particular skills and knowledge—the price is less autonomy. Furthermore, in some instances, group work is more time-consuming and requires added energy relative to keeping everyone on the same page and the need to continually negotiate to maintain a balance and keep the focus on the task at hand. Personal strengths and weaknesses often present difficult challenges relative to reaching a group consensus.

With these pros and cons in mind listed above in mind, what are some advantages and disadvantages for anthropologists generally and yourself specifically working in groups? A disadvantage of group work for anthropologists is that the entire outcome is often viewed as the direct result of a collaborative effort; therefore, not enough emphasis may be paid to individuals' contributions, advances in their own expertise, or what credit they should each receive for new knowledge gained. As stated above, group work requires not only giving up of control and the expenditure of greater amount of time (and perhaps energy), but often requires the anthropologist to put aside her personal agenda or research interests for the benefit of the group process.

Advantages of group work lay in the added support of colleagues, the ability of being able to "see" different perspectives and view concepts and theories through various lenses, to test your own theories in a collaborative environment, and to garner support for either expanding or refuting current theories and methodologies.

On a personal level, I view group work as an opportunity to increase my understanding of the entire process of conducting research, to learn new skills and enhance my knowledge relative to applying theories and methodologies. My main challenge with group work is the constant need to negotiate and renegotiate the direction of the project—to keep all members of the group in focus and moving toward the same goal. Additionally, due to my innate desire for excellence in all things attempted, I tend to be one to take charge; thereby (at least in my mind) ensuring the project process and outcome adheres to the highest standards.

Step 2 (see Table II.6.2 on the following page)

Terri Ann's Self-Reflection Participating in this team research project provided the opportunity for me to utilize my management skills while making me aware of the special considerations inherent in conducting research from a collaborative perspective. Individuals are naturally curious and sometimes sensitive beings—novice anthropologists tend to present as individuals who are struggling with not only "finding themselves" in the world of anthropology but also so eager to learn and share their new-found knowledge. Group work thus lends itself to the creation of environments that stimulate the desire to seek out new ways of knowing, to try out new ideas while pressing individuals to maintain their uniqueness, at the same time reinforcing the notion that collective knowledge may be the basis or foundation of greater things to come.

The value-added of this experience and the enhancement of my anthropological skills enable me to seek out opportunities whereby I can utilize these skills in the context of working on other collaborative projects such as research assistant positions or seeking out other group research projects. But probably most important is the self-confidence gained from actually "doing" a research project.

Table II.6.2.   Terri Ann's Reflections on Working Collaboratively

Project Description	My Role	Key Insights	Suggestions for Future Group Work
Hunters and Gatherers at Wayne State An advanced research methods class group project involving designing, implementing, and analyzing data from a Rapid Ethnographic Assessment of the food preferences, sources, policies, and practices of WSU students	Observation Team Leader Detail-oriented Note-taker Facilitated task management and communicated with other team leaders	(1) How to conduct observations, (2) benefits of mapping observation site, (3) project management, (4) enhanced communication skills relative to achieving consensus, (5) conflict resolution, (6) adjusting to in-group changes—constant fluctuation of team membership, (7) reinforcement of importance of "taking charge"	In hindsight—I realized that I am quite comfortable in the leadership role. In future group situations, I would simply step up initially to the leadership role. But also in retrospect, while working from a collaborative position, I would still assert a democratic approach, but I would pay closer attention to group dynamics and possibly do more assigning of tasks and responsibilities based on individual member's abilities and skill sets
Time line—7 weeks Conducted as part of ANT 7200 class—10 students (novice anthropologists) divided into 3 research teams: A) Interview Team B) Observation Team, and C) History and Text Team Primary mode of communication: weekly face-to-face meetings and email	Assumed leadership role after original leader dropped the class, with the support of the other members		

EXERCISE 7

Understanding Your Personal and Professional Balance

The Lifestyle Exercise

Activity Overview

This exercise will help you consider the right balance of personal and professional activities in your life. Some people are comfortable when much overlap exists between work and leisure realms. For instance, there are anthropologists who conduct ethnographic research for their jobs and like to read ethnographies in their spare time. Others prefer to keep work and leisure time more separate and distinct. Thinking consciously about what is the optimal arrangement for you can help you mover closer to achieving it. You will go through several comparative steps below to help you think deeply about these issues.

Instructions

Step 1

Initially, make the circle on the following page into a pie chart by drawing lines to divide it into what percentages of your time you wish to devote to particular personal and professional activities. You can divide the pie chart into as many categories as you like. For example, percentage for time spent with family, friends, hobbies, community activities (e.g., volunteering), work projects, getting advanced training (such as in languages or software usage). We recommend using pencil to do this task so that you can possibly change and redraw these lines a few different times as you go through the exercise.

Step 2

Create two schedules: one will envision what your ideal daily schedule would look like, and one will represent what your actual daily schedule is

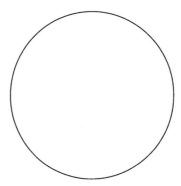

like by assigning different personal and professional activities to various time slots. The examples in Tables II.7.1 and II.7.2 are provided to help you organize your thoughts for subsequently comparing the ideal with the real. If an activity extends over multiple time slots, draw a line through the ones that follow until the activity would end. Alternatively, if you are more comfortable doing so, you can write a narrative description for each day in which you detail the activities one by one, but keep in mind that the ultimate goal is to be able to directly compare the ideal and real day's schedules.

Step 3

Put your ideal and actual days' schedules side by side. Look at each and consider how they match up. To what extent are you surprised or not by what you see? Now go back and compare with your pie-chart diagram from Step 1. Again, to what extent are you surprised or not by what you see? Are these results what you envisioned they would be for an anthropologically oriented career? Why or why not? Based on this comparison create an action plan that would enable you to take steps to get closer to the balance you seek.

Table 7.1 Sample Ideal Day

Time	Activity	Where Done	Personal Activity, Professional Activity, or Both?	Notes
12:00 AM	Sleep	Home	Personal	
1:00 AM				
2:00 AM				
3:00 AM				
4:00 AM				
5:00 AM				
6:00 AM	Childcare	Home	Both	Had some fun play time in the morning with my kid
7:00 AM				
8:00 AM	Check and return email	Home	Both	Read all of my messages
9:00 AM	Finish writing book and submit to editor	Home	Professional	I got this project finished!
10:00 AM				
11:00 AM				
12:00 PM	Lunch	Home	Personal	
1:00 PM	Drive to office, Listen to audiobook on CD	On the road	Both	Felt relaxed during car ride
2:00 PM	Teach an anthropology class	Work	Professional	Great class
3:00 PM				
4:00 PM	Hold office hours	Work	Professional	Good meetings with students
5:00 PM	Work out	Gym	Personal	Felt fit and accomplished
6:00 PM	Drive home, Listen to audiobook on CD	On the road	Both	Felt relaxed during car ride
7:00 PM	Make dinner/ Childcare	Home	Personal	Tasty, quick home-cooked meal, then story-time with my kid
8:00 PM				
9:00 PM	Read book for fun	Home	Personal	Got back to that exciting novel I've been wanting to finish
10:00 PM	Bedtime	Home	Personal	Ready to rest following a great, productive day
11:00 PM				

Table II.7.2. Sample Actual Day

Time	Activity	Where Done	Personal Task, Professional Task, or Both?	Notes
12:00 AM	Sleep	Home	Personal	
1:00 AM				
2:00 AM				
3:00 AM				
4:00 AM				
5:00 AM	Childcare	Home	Both	Tired, felt rushed to get ready
6:00 AM				
7:00 AM	Check and return email	Home	Both	Baby napping so I can work at my desk
8:00 AM				
9:00 AM	Writing	Home	Professional	Can't finish e-mail, switch over to writing try to meet pending book deadline
10:00 AM				
11:00 AM				
12:00 PM	Lunch	Home	Personal	
1:00 PM	Drive to office		Professional	Bad traffic, very stressful
2:00 PM	Hold office hours	Work	Professional	Was late for my first meeting of the day
3:00 PM				
4:00 PM				
5:00 PM	Drive home		Professional	I wish I had time to work out today
6:00 PM	Make dinner/ Childcare	Home	Personal	
7:00 PM				
8:00 PM				
9:00 PM	Check and return emails	Home	Both	Still can't finish answering e-mails
10:00 PM	Housework and preparing for next day	Home	Both	Wish I had some "down time" to relax for myself
11:00 PM	Bedtime	Home	Personal	

Self-Reflection

Write one or two paragraphs about what you learned about how you manage your work and personal lives from doing this exercise. How motivated are you to keep things as they are or readjust the balance in some ways? What do you see as the likelihood that you will make changes in the near future or later on? What would it take for you to make these changes? Imagine if you did this exercise again ten years from now, in what ways might you expect the results to be different?

Follow-Up Activities

- Find someone in your life with a good work/life balance that you admire. Ask him or her about his or her ideal and actual days, and how this person achieves balance in his or her life. Find an anthropologist to do the same step with, if the first person you selected was not an anthropologist.
- Try using your ideal schedule as though it were your actual schedule for one week. Think about what insights you gained about achieving balance in your work and personal life by doing this experiment.

| Sample Exercise Completed by Marlo, a Ph.D. Student |

Step 1 (Figure II.7.1)

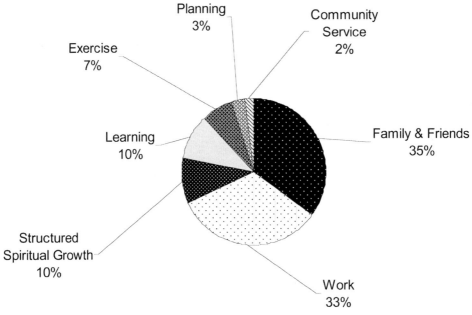

Figure II.7.1

Step 2 (see Tables II.7.3 and II.7.4 on pages 85 and 86, which are this student's ideal and actual days)

Table II.7.3. Marlo's Ideal Day

Time	Activity	Where Done	Personal Activity, Professional Activity, or Both?	Notes
12:00 AM	Sleep	Home	Personal	
1:00 AM				
2:00 AM				
3:00 AM				
4:00 AM				
5:00 AM	Meditate, dress			
6:00 AM	Childcare	Home	Personal	Do Mali's hair, help to prepare her to go
	Drive to gym/ listen to spiritual or business CD	On the Road	Personal	
7:00 AM	Workout	Gym	Personal	
8:00 AM				
9:00 AM				
	Get dressed			
10:00 AM	Work	Office	Office	
11:00 AM				
12:00 PM	Lunch			
1:00 PM	Work			
2:00 PM				
3:00 PM				
4:00 PM				
5:00 PM	Pick up Mali and drive home/ listen to spiritual or business CD	On the road	Both	I like using the 40 minute commute to learn
6:00 PM	Make dinner/time with Mali and Charles	Home	Personal	Good time for family to interact
7:00 PM				
8:00 PM				
9:00 PM	Put Mali to bed, time w/Charles, learning or planning			Good time for accomplishing things; couple time
10:00 PM	Bedtime	Home	Personal	Go to sleep rather than falling asleep at my desk
11:00 PM				

Table II.7.4. Marlo's Actual Day

Time	Activity	Where Done	Personal Activity, Professional Activity, or Both?	Notes
12:00 AM	Sleep	Home	Personal	
1:00 AM				
2:00 AM				
3:00 AM				
4:00 AM				
5:00 AM				Don't wake up early enough for meditation
6:00 AM	Dress/Childcare			Do Mali's hair, help to prepare her to go
	Drive to gym/ listen to spiritual or business CD	On the Road	Personal	
7:00 AM	Workout	Gym	Personal	
8:00 AM				
9:00 AM	Get dressed			
	Work	Office	Office	
10:00 AM				
11:00 AM				
12:00 PM	Lunch			
1:00 PM	Work			
2:00 PM				
3:00 PM				
4:00 PM				
5:00 PM				
6:00 PM	Pick up Mali and drive home/ listen to spiritual or business CD	On the road	Both	I have not gotten the spiritual CDs; I get home later than I want
7:00 PM	Make dinner/time with Mali and Charles	Home	Personal	I don't get home in time to cook for Charles
8:00 PM				
9:00 PM	Put Mali to bed; Work on learning or planning	Home	Personal	I rarely make the time to be with Charles in an engaged way
10:00 PM				I stay up late working on school/ other assignments
11:00 PM				

Marlo's Self-Reflection   I know that this exercise reflects my weekday life, which is significantly different from my weekend life. That being said, upon examination, my life is reasonably close to my ideal. I like the idea of fewer work hours, but I also really like my job, which currently demands my full-time presence. There are a few simple things I can do to better balance my life—go to bed earlier and rise earlier, get spiritual CDs, structure ways for Charles and I to spend time together—a game night, for example, cook meals on the weekends to eat on the weekdays. I feel frantic juggling everything, even when I don't have a great deal to juggle in a particular moment. Sometimes just the thought of caring for a thirteen-month-old, working a full-time job, planning a wedding, and earning my doctorate simultaneously is overwhelming.

I am motivated to handle the simple things soon though, because I know my life works well when these things are in place. I will also position myself to work fewer hours for more money. It feels great to spend a lot of time with Mali and Charles in the morning—or working out, rather than rushing off to the job. I want to be an academic entrepreneur (professor with a supplementary "lifestyle" business) for that reason. Ideally, I want the stability, prestige, and flexibility of a university setting with the compensation of the private sector.

EXERCISE 8

Understanding Your Advising Relationships

The Mentorship Exercise

Activity Overview

The main goals of this exercise are to think about and create a meaningful, personal definition of mentorship and then develop strategies for achieving such a mentoring relationship. A mentor can be a boss, professor, friend, parent, role model, or spiritual advisor. The mentoring relationship can be cordial, formal, personal, professional, or informal. Ideally though a successful mentor will be someone whose judgment you trust and advice you seek. You can be mentored by someone, and you can be a mentor to another person. As you develop your personal definition, you will learn more about what you are looking for in a mentorship relationship.

Instructions

Step 1

Write one to two paragraphs to answer each set of questions below and explore your own ideas and needs in a mentoring relationship. It may be easier to first get your ideas down on paper in a series of bullet points and then write them out and reorganize them in a narrative format.

Who:
• Who would you like to be your mentor?

- What personal characteristics should that person have?

- What professional connections does this person have that could help you?

- Describe the relationship you would like to have.

What:
- What are your expectations of the mentoring relationship?

- What will you and your mentor do together or talk about?

- Will you talk about academic advising, ask for career advice, intellectual guidance, personal encouragement, or ethical advice?

Where:
- Where will you and your mentor meet?

- Will you meet in person or over the phone?

- Will you use communication technologies, such as email, instant messaging, or chat?

When:
- How often do you meet?

- Under what circumstances?

- In what ways is your mentor accessible, willing, and able?

- How will you set a schedule so both of your needs are met?

- How much advance notice will your mentor need to be able to schedule a meeting with you?

- Do you need an agenda in order to have a meeting you both feel will be successful? Or can you simply meet anytime to "touch base" more casually?

Why:
- Why would this relationship be good for you and for my mentor?

- What can you both teach and learn from the partnership?

- What are the mutual benefits as well as the individual benefits?

Step 2

Create a meaningful personal definition of mentorship and define who you imagine your mentor to be by drawing upon all of these different points. Share this definition with your current classmates or other people in your life and get their feedback.

Step 3

Compare your personal definition with a mentoring relationship you already have and see to what degree the ideal and real characteristics correspond.

Self-Reflection

Write a paragraph or two reflecting on the experience of doing this exercise. Discuss what you have discovered about how you view mentoring relationships and contemplate how you will make use of this knowledge in the future. For example, you may consider here how you imagine your mentorship needs will change over time as you move forward in your career development. Consider to what extent it may or may not be important for you to have a mentor who is an anthropologist at various stages of your career.

Follow-Up Activities

- Discuss your mentorship ideas with someone you would like to be mentored by, using the attributes you listed above to see if there is a mutual fit and benefit.
- Do some research on organizations you are interested in or belong to and see if there is a mentoring option there. You could also request to be mentored by someone in that organization or even volunteer to be a mentor.

Sample Exercise Completed by Elizabeth, a Ph.D. Student

Step 1

Who: Ideally, I would like to have a mentor who can help me to successfully develop as a scholar and who can help me transition while going through the Ph.D. process and then afterward. My mentor would possess personal characteristics that would demonstrate skill and knowledge as well as good motivation strategies. Other personal characteristics that I would like my mentor to possess include: good boundaries, honesty, intellect, confidence, and kindness. I believe that these kinds of characteristics are essential to being a good leader and teacher. Furthermore, these kinds of skills make for good personal and professional connections—I would like to know that my mentor has good connections in academia and industry. Ultimately, I would like a relationship that is mutually beneficial—I want to learn from and be supported by my mentor and I want to assist my mentor in his or her scholarly endeavors (e.g., research). I would like a mentoring relationship where I am encouraged to ask questions and where I am pushed to think through things in novel ways.

What: My expectations for a mentoring relationship are that we would be a good match personally and academically, that we would set goals and expectations, and that we would communicate openly. Generally, we would share ideas and work toward conducting research projects, including literature reviews, methods/procedural development, analysis, and writing. We would also spend some time at professional/social events where I could observe and interact with colleagues and potential colleagues. I would like to be able to ask my mentor for academic advice and to gain intellectual/professional guidance.

Where: Generally, my mentor and I would meet on campus at a university building or restaurant/coffee shop. Other venues for meetings might include industry sites, our homes, or public places. My preference for meetings would be in person. Telephone and email communications would also occur. However, I believe that face-to-face meetings are beneficial.

When: Depending on whether or not we are working on a research project, we might meet a few times a week to once or twice a month. I would expect that while working on a project we would meet more frequently—and that we would meet more frequently in the beginning and a little less as I develop the skills to conduct work on my own. In terms of availability, my mentor and I would need to negotiate this. I am not sure right now what kind of time/schedule we would work out. To create a schedule that would meet both of our needs, we would need to talk first and define the scope of our relationship/project. I think that there would be times where we would need an agenda to stay on track. However, I envision that most of the time we would meet on a more casual basis and take good notes to keep track of progress, limitations, emergent questions, results, insights, and so forth.

Why: I consider the mentor/mentee relationship to be mutually beneficial in terms of transitions—mentees are in transition, moving from one place in the world to another, while mentors are in transition as they become leaders (or hone leadership skills) who help their mentee(s) develop skills and knowledge.

Step 2

Working definition: A mentor helps their mentee to develop knowledge and skills that will help each propel toward greater success in life processes such as school or professional work. Success may build on work already in progress or help during transitional times. Mentors are socially and professionally connected—they are able to help mentees develop relationships and the skills to successfully leverage those relationships. There are clear goals and a schedule that guides the relationship. At the same time, these boundaries are flexible. As opportunities and challenges arise, the mentor and mentee must also learn how to engage and negotiate the unexpected. Ultimately, the relationship should be built on good intentions for a long-term relationship that will be mutually beneficial.

Feedback: I did talk with a few friends about this project/definition. I did not really get much feedback other than short phrases like, *sounds good*.

Step 3

I do not currently have a mentoring relationship. Actually, I have never had a formal mentoring relationship.

Elizabeth's Self-Reflection   I had to imagine my answers because I do not have a mentoring relationship and am not really seeking one. But I would like a mentoring relationship. During this process I wondered why I have not sought a mentor out. I think that I feel really insecure and like no one would want to mentor me. And I thought about my role as a mentor for WSU's Urban Scholars—nontraditional undergraduate students who are active volunteers in their communities but who do not consistently perform well academically. For the first time, I realized that I am a little like this. Many of us (mentors) have discussed the possibility that the students need more social mentorship to be more successful with professors and peers from more "traditional" backgrounds. I wonder now if the Scholars have trouble asking for, maybe knowing what/how to ask for, guidance in the places they want to go/be. How can you envision something unseen and so foreign? I see that people are successful in academia and in industry, but I don't know the questions to ask or the ways to attain that success. I feel confident that I can meet some academic challenges, but beyond that, I just don't know where to begin or how to get to where I see other people.

I think that it will take me some time to think about all of this and to develop my thoughts on mentoring. This exercise is very good because we all need to be thinking about these things so that we have agency and the ability to develop our own visions. Currently, the Urban Scholars' Program is very top-down. But none of us know what our mentees hope for. For now, we get paired up depending on our academic discipline. This exercise would be really great for mentees to work through so that we could be better paired—and I think that mentors need to work through ideas about their/our roles as well.

I think that it is vital for me to develop a mentoring relationship with an anthropologist in order to become an anthropologist. Right now I feel like I'm floating around a bit and that maybe I should transition to another department or school. At the moment, I feel like the closest thing I have to developing a mentoring relationship is in the College of Engineering. And this is potentially very good for work in industry. But I would prefer to make a career in academia. I'm just not sure how to ask the right questions, seek out the right people, and, well, move forward.

Follow-Up Activities

I did not do the follow-up activities as I was not ready to approach someone as a potential (formal) mentor. I think that it will take me time to think more about the questions raised in this exercise and to develop a vision of what I want and where I want to go.

EXERCISE 9

Understanding Your Professional Connections

The Networking Exercise

Activity Overview

Networking is an important activity at any stage of your career. You might have a general idea of what kinds of work you want to do but not know about the variety of jobs and how people have forged career paths in these areas. Getting started, networking will help you to meet a series of people who can assist you in designing your career. Later on, networking can help you to expand the range of people you know and uncover additional kinds of opportunities you have to employ your anthropological skills. Although many implicitly know there is value in networking, this exercise is designed to help you explicitly think about some steps you can take in building a professional network of people who can help you build and move forward in your career.

Instructions

Step 1

Identify some general goals for your networking strategy. Answer the questions below or create your own networking goals.

- What kinds of people do I want to meet?

- What do I want to learn from these people for my career development?

- Other networking goals.

Step 2

Make your own version of Table II.9.1 to more specifically define what kinds of networking encounters you would like to have. Try to be specific here—what would you want to learn from these people and what do you think they can offer that would be helpful to you? Similarly, what can you exchange with them in return?

Table II.9.1. Defining Networking Encounters

Type of Person	*Characteristics*	*What I Would Like to Learn*	*What I Can Offer*
Senior anthropologist who knows about working as a curator	1. Employed in a museum now 2. Teaches museum studies	1. Job opportunities in this specialized field 2. What training/experience required (both on paper) and what makes one competitive for this kind of position? 3. Who could I meet working in this area now?	Up-to-date knowledge of how training for this specialization is occurring at the masters' degree level Willingness to work in entry level position in this area

Step 3

Develop an action plan to meet one or more of each kind of person you identified in the table. Think about how you will locate these people (e.g., ask my advisor, look on the Internet, contact a local organization, attend a national conference, etc.). Will you initially contact them by email, phone, mail? What kinds of follow-up will you need to do once you have established your initial connections and after you have made contact with these people?

Self-Reflection

Write one or two paragraphs reflecting on the experience of doing this exercise. Discuss what you have discovered about the professional network you would like to have and your strategy for creating it. What steps will you need to take to maintain and further cultivate your network in the future? How do you think your networking strategy may change over time as you progress in your career?

Follow-Up Activities

- Make a list of standard and individualized questions you want to ask the various people you plan to network with.
- Consider what kinds of materials would be useful to have for networking with these people (e.g., business cards, resumé, portfolio). Generate any of these materials that you do not already have.
- Contemplate which people in your life you regard as those who could help you to increase your network over time. Take into account family, friends, neighbors, former and current teachers, bosses, colleagues, people who are alumni of your school, people who belong to the same community groups, congregations, volunteer organizations, and so forth. Think about your network very broadly here!

Sample Exercise Completed by Lindsey, a Ph.D. Student

Step 1

- *What kinds of people do I want to meet?*
  Medical anthropologists working in the public health field.

- *What do I want to learn from these people for my career development?*
  What role a medical anthropologist can play in multidisciplinary and interdisciplinary teams working in the area of public health.

- *Other Networking Goals:*
  To make contacts with others from different disciplines, but have the same research/career interests.

Step 2 (see Table II.9.2 on the following page, which is this student's model).

Table II.9.2. Lindsey's Sample Networking Goals

Type of Person	Characteristics	What I Would Like to Learn	What I Can Offer
Medical anthropologists working in a health agency	1. Employed in a large health agency such as the Centers for Disease Control (CDC) or National Institutes of Health (NIH). 2. Currently working as part of a multidisciplinary research team in a public health oriented agency.	1. What can medical anthropologists offer working in these types of agencies? 2. What is it like working in this type of environment? 3. What skills do I need to work in this type of setting (specific qualitative and quantitative skills)? 4. Are there post-doc training opportunities available?	Solid background in qualitative research methods and working knowledge of quantitative methods. Graduate certification in public health. Knowledge of culture, health and illness.

Step 3

Action plan: The first step in my action plan will be to compile a list of people I hope to contact in order to learn more about working as a medical anthropologist in a large public health–oriented setting. I will develop this list by talking with my advisor and other faculty to inquire if they have contacts in such agencies or if they know of someone who has contacts in these agencies. I will also research the websites of various agencies and locate individuals who are anthropologists or have similar research interests. I will then initially contact these individuals on my list by email. If initial contact is successful, I will try to arrange a meeting either via phone or during a conference to further discuss my interests. I will also directly network at anthropology conferences, especially those conferences that focus on the applied aspects of the field (e.g., the Society for Applied Anthropology). I will attend interest group meetings to meet possible contacts and visit the exhibition floor to meet representatives from these agencies to obtain additional contact information.

Lindsey's Self-Reflection   I originally found the prospect of creating a professional network overwhelming. This exercise really helped me focus on specific career goals and what steps I need to take to achieve these goals. Creating an action plan helped take the fear out of the networking process. I have often worried about how to go about approaching an individual in order to inquire about his or her career. Taking networking step by step I think will help students build more confidence to approach individuals they want to talk to and to ask key questions to help make their career choices a reality. With this exercise, I began to realize that a network is essential to help "get your foot in the door" in a competitive job market.

I believe that ongoing contact will be essential in maintaining and cultivating my network. This ongoing contact I think will be important in remaining up to date on developments in my chosen field and possible job/training opportunities. My goal is to continually build this network as my contacts introduce me to others in the field. I think that over time, my networking strategy may change. I think gaining work experience will give me more confidence to expand my network beyond the boundaries of my field and engage in collaborative relationships with individuals in other fields, but with similar research interests.

EXERCISE 10

Understanding Your Ideal Job

The Anthropological Job Search Exercise

Activity Overview

You have begun to explore the universe of possibilities for the kind of work you want to do through previous exercises considering your work and academic experiences and learning to translate these into anthropological skills that employers will find valuable. Additionally, you have considered what is most important to you on personal and professional levels and how to meet people who can help you. Now you will imagine what ideal jobs would be, see what jobs exist that are like that, and match your skills to them. Once you see the range of job possibilities calling for your skill set, you can actively pursue your anthropologically oriented career path.

Instructions

Step 1

Create a job advertisement that describes your ideal job. Typical job advertisements have a description of the duties of the job, the skills required for the job, and other requirements, such as degrees or ability to travel. Write out a job advertisement that portrays your ideal job situation.

Step 2

Define your position objective in one or two sentences, maximum. Succinctly state what position you are looking for, such as a position working with seniors, or a position that allows you to use your anthropology background.

Step 3

Make a table of organizations, types of positions you are interested in applying to, and the skills required for each position. Use job search sites such as monster.com, careerbuilder.com, and the like to help you find types of organizations you would like to work for. You can search by keyword, so you can search for jobs that have a requirement of a degree in anthropology, or experience with ethnography, or qualitative research methods, for example. This search method will unearth organizations and jobs you may not have considered before. Your table could look like the sample Table II.10.1.

Table II.10.1. Sample Table of Possible Anthropology-Related Jobs

Organization	Position	Skills Required for Position	Skills Matched
Long-term care facility	Recreation coordinator	Bachelor's degree—relevant field	BA in anthropology
		Program development experience	Was program director in previous job
		Supervisory experience	Supervised one other team member
Oral history society	Project interviewer	Experience with one-on-one interviewing	Independently managed and conducted an oral history project in a class
		Data collection and data management skills (e.g., ability to use qualitative software for coding interviews)	Used Atlas.ti for data management and analysis
Social service agency	Senior center program planner	Bachelor's degree—relevant field	BA in anthropology
		Experience working with older adults (several years desired)	Volunteered at senior center for two years during college
		Verbal and written communication skills	Received grant award
		Organizational skills Interpersonal skills Grant writing skills	Project management experience

Step 4

Articulate the key qualities that make you a perfect candidate for each job you found by matching the skills required to skills you have. Go back to your earlier exercises to help you. When writing a cover letter or email, use the descriptions of how your skills match the skills required to articulate why you are qualified for the job.

Self-Reflection

Write a paragraph or two about your experience matching your anthropological skills to jobs you found and comparing to the ideal job you envisioned for yourself. In what ways is this exercise similar or different to how you have found jobs in the past? Is the process in this exercise easier or more difficult than you expected? How so? How do you envision your ideal job and related job search changing over time? For example, how do you imagine it might be different one year from now or ten years from now?

Follow-Up Activities

- Develop a schedule for regularly checking job search sites and other venues where you are likely to be able to find jobs in your chosen area. Repeat this process of filling in the categories given on the table to be aware of what opportunities exist in fields of interest to you and what job qualifications well-suited applicants are supposed to possess.
- Try this process with your past work and volunteer experiences. Does it help you articulate skills you didn't know you had?

Sample Exercise Completed by Amy, a Ph.D. Student

Step 1—Ideal Job Description

Wanted: Experienced researcher with a passion for solving problems to plan and lead research projects for new product design. Work directly with clients to assess needs and develop projects. Conduct research with interdisciplinary team members to collect qualitative and quantitative data to provide analysis and insight for new product design. Must be familiar with qualitative and quantitative methods of data collection. Also must be proficient in Mac and PC software use. Advanced degree and relevant work experience (5+ years) required. Travel approximately 25%.

Step 2—Position Objective

I am seeking a position that allows me to solve problems with actionable insights derived from anthropological methods of data collection and analysis. I have the ability to work independently or cooperatively in cross-functional teams to meet project deadlines, work with clients, and exceed goals.

Steps 3 and 4 (see Table II.10.2 on the following pages, which is this student's model)

Table II.10.2. Amy's Possible Anthropology-Related Jobs

Organization	Position	Skills Required for Position	Skills Matched
Design company	Human factors specialist	Expertise in managing and coordinating projects such as participant recruiting efforts both internally and with outside participant recruiting agencies.	I have recruited participants on my own for independent research projects, and I have used a professional recruiter as part of my experience working for a design company.
		Natural talent for understanding human-centered design issues and a desire to learn more about the methodology.	I had an internship with a design company, so I had the opportunity to demonstrate anthropological methods and I learned.how to translate analysis into design principles.
		Able to handle pressure, short deadlines, and time-sensitive projects.	
		Qualified candidates should be familiar with Microsoft Word, Excel, Powerpoint, InDesign. FileMaker Pro, or other database knowledge is a plus.	I have experience with all of the programs mentioned, and my educational background is from anthropology.
		Background in social science desired.	My passion is doing the research in order to develop better products.
Marketing research company	Project director	Passion for marketing research.	I have more than five years' experience in a variety of work contexts.
		Minimum two years research experience.	
		Aptitude for custom research design, execution and analysis.	I can demonstrate with previous projects my experience with research design, execution, and analysis.
		Excellent client management skills.	I have worked directly with clients.
		Ability to multitask and effectively manage deadlines.	I can give examples from my jobs where I had to manage deadlines and do multiple tasks simultaneously.

(continued)

Table II.10.2. *(continued)*

Organization	Position	Skills Required for Position	Skills Matched
Ice cream company	Consumer market insight analyst	Identify new product/innovation and brand communication opportunities.	I can draw from my work experiences to talk about new product development, and the process of reaching consumers to develop deeper understanding.
		Manage primary consumer research projects, both qualitative and quantitative, for assigned brands. This research will span consumer attitudes and usage, advertising development and copy testing, new product concept development and new product evaluation, consumer segmentation, and ethnography.	I know about ethnography and some of the methods for data gathering.
		Present research insights to the senior management team, marketing department, and others in the company as needed.	I have experience presenting findings to key stakeholders and also in training others on software.
		Train marketing or other staff in the use of all available analytical software, tools, and standard reports.	
		Advanced degree in marketing, marketing research, or social science preferred 20% travel	My degree matches, as does my desire to travel!

Amy's Self-Reflection   I feel like I have always known that I wanted to work in industry after finishing my Ph.D. Writing the ideal job description was fairly easy because I have had a lot of diverse work experiences along the way, so I can reflect on the best parts of the jobs I've had and combine them into one ideal position.

The first two jobs in the table are from companies that I plan to apply to when I graduate, because I know the kind of work they do and I know that someone with my background and skills would easily fit in there. I went right to the company websites and searched their current job openings and added them to the table. Then, I searched monster.com using the keyword "ethnography" to find any jobs that had that word in the job description. The ice cream job just jumped out at me, because I love ice cream! When matching my skills to the job requirements, I drew upon all of my various work experiences to illustrate how I am prepared for the jobs that appeal to me. The ice cream job requests specific marketing knowledge, which I don't have, but describing how I can do the job with my anthropological skills and business experience will make up for that lack.

As my academic preparation comes to an end, I am thinking ahead to the kind of work I want to do. I will do this exercise once I am ready to enter the job market, and I would definitely do this exercise when I'm ready to change jobs or take the next step in my anthropological career, because I see how it helps me organize my thinking and target what kind of job I want.

EXERCISE 11

Representing Yourself Professionally as an Anthropologist

The Introduction Exercise

Activity Overview

This exercise will teach you how to introduce yourself in a way that ties together your background, skills, and experiences in a way that makes sense for the listener. The goal is to have modular pieces you can move around and interchange depending on who you are talking to. Consider what order you put things in because you do not know how much time you have with someone. Keep in mind people are most likely to remember the first and last things they hear, and plan the order of what you will say accordingly.

Instructions

Step 1

Create three versions of a professional introduction. Consider the amount and type of information going into different length introductions. Keep your language simple so that people can easily understand what you are saying. Develop modular pieces so that you can highlight different components of your story to suit any situation.

> *Version 1:* The first introduction is good for a quick situation, such as when you are in an elevator and you only have twenty or so seconds to make a connection before you arrive at your destination.
> *Version 2:* The second introduction will be useful when you are talking to a very busy person but you need to convey some sense of your background or experience.
> *Version 3:* The third introduction will serve when you are talking with someone who is quite interested in your background and you need to provide the details of your experience clearly and succinctly.

Hopefully, in each of these cases, the person you are speaking with will be intrigued enough to ask you more questions and have the conversation go further!

Next we include examples of a student and a midcareer anthropologist's introductions to give you some ideas about how you might put versions of your own introduction together.

Step 2

Try out your introductions with friends, family, or coworkers to see if your versions make sense. Sometimes what sounds good on paper does not make sense or is hard to understand when spoken. Those who know you best will have some helpful feedback for you so you can edit your introductions to be even better. Have them introduce themselves to you, so you can hear how other people from other professional backgrounds tailor their information to their listeners. Edit your introductions as necessary.

Self-Reflection

How has this exercise helped you view yourself? Do you find yourself thinking differently about your anthropological career or how to talk about it? Do you have a perspective on how your professional introductions might change over the long term? If so, how? Write a paragraph or two explaining what you learned from this assignment.

Follow-Up Activities

- Practice your introductions often so you have no hesitation when you are in the right situation. You could practice in the shower or when you are driving.
- Write out or type your introductions on a three-by-five card to carry in your book bag, or print them on a business card–sized piece of sturdy paper for your wallet so you can refer to them quickly and easily.

Samples Completed by the Authors:
Example of a Student's Introduction Versions

Version 1: Hello, my name is Amy Goldmacher. I'm a research assistant in the Department of Industrial/Manufacturing Engineering at Wayne State University in Detroit. I'm not an engineer, however; I'm finishing my master's degree in anthropology, and my main interest is business anthropology.

I would use this version if I were being quickly introduced to someone who needed to know what I did. I could modify this piece and simply say that I was completing my MA in Anthropology and leave out the Engineering part.

Version 2: Hello, my name is Amy Goldmacher. I'm a research assistant in the Department of Industrial/Manufacturing Engineering at Wayne State University in Detroit. I'm not an engineer, however; I'm finishing my master's degree in anthropology. I get asked all the time, "What's an anthropologist doing in the Engineering Department?" I usually say that as a business anthropologist, I use the tools and methods of cultural anthropology, such as ethnography and participant observation, in business settings to gather qualitative and quantitative data for analysis.

I would use this version if I were being introduced to nonanthropologists who needed an explanation of what business anthropology is, because few people know about this subfield.

Version 3: Hello, my name is Amy Goldmacher. I'm a research assistant in the Department of Industrial/Manufacturing Engineering at Wayne State University in Detroit. I'm not an engineer, however; I'm finishing my master's degree in anthropology. I get asked all the time, "What's an anthropologist doing in the Engineering Department?" I usually say that as a business anthropologist, I use the tools and methods of cultural anthropology, such as ethnography and participant observation, in business settings to gather qualitative and quantitative data for analysis. An example of the kind of work I do is a project I did with automotive executives, where I assessed the effectiveness of training engineers on a new cost reduction system.

I would use this version if I were introducing myself to nonanthropologists who needed to know something about my background or experience. I have used this introduction when I am doing work for clients as a way of "justifying my existence" in engineering and explaining why an anthropologist can make a useful contribution. If a person is quite interested, I could build on the project example and explain more about what the analysis revealed, or I could use a different project if it were more suitable.

Example of a Mid-Career Anthropologist's Introduction Versions

Version 1: Hello. I'm Sherylyn Briller—a medical anthropologist who specializes in cultural issues relating to health and aging.

I would use this version if I am introducing myself to someone in a quick situation (e.g., waiting in line to buy coffee in the morning at a professional conference). If I were using this version in settings with nonanthropologists, I might define medical anthropology or tell them that I was a gerontologist instead. If I wanted to simplify the message, I would say that I'm someone who works in the area of aging research and policy—or just say that I've worked for fifteen years with older adults.

Version 2: Hello. I'm Dr. Sherylyn Briller—a medical anthropologist who specializes in cultural issues relating to health and aging. My research has focused on old-age support and end-of-life issues. I've worked in the United States and in Asia.

I would use this version for a very brief introduction when I am giving an academic or policy-related talk. Similarly, I might use this introduction if I were giving a sound byte for the media and needed to explain my credentials. Also this version could be used as a "bio" statement if I wrote a book chapter and needed to summarize my work in a couple of sentences.

Version 3: Good afternoon. I'm Dr. Sherylyn Briller—a medical anthropologist who specializes in cultural issues relating to health and aging. My dissertation research examined family and governmental old-age support mechanisms as well as the impact of rapid societal change on the elderly in Mongolia. In the United States, I have significant experience conducting research in long-term care, focusing on creating more successful dementia-care settings. My current research agenda focuses on end-of-life care issues, and I have several different funded projects in this area.

I would use this version if I were introducing myself to people who are quite interested in my background—including my international and domestic research background. On the first day of class for example, I would use this introduction to explain my professional background to the students. If I were "pitching" a consulting job, I would further customize this version to emphasize areas that closely fit with a potential client's needs. I would provide more detailed information about whatever pieces are most relevant for the audience at hand (e.g., research methodologies, summary of findings, a concise explanation of the added value of having an anthropologist work on an interdisciplinary team and so forth).

EXERCISE 12

Representing Yourself in a Summary Document

The Resumé Exercise

Activity Overview

A resumé is a short, one- or two-page biographical document that summarizes your educational and work background. Often, people get nervous when it is time to write a resumé, but you should view this task as your chance to create a road map of your career. This activity will help you review your accomplishments and think about where you want to go next. Most job seekers have a *chronological resumé*, which lists their experiences going backward in time from the present to the earliest ones. For an anthropological career search, you may also want to have a *functional resumé*, which would group experiences into sets of professional skills (e.g., interpersonal skills, technical skills, and so forth). Although the chronological resumé remains most commonly used, the functional resumé can also be useful for those with diverse backgrounds, such as anthropologists. Job seekers early in their careers typically will use the chronological resumé, which best encapsulates the entire range of jobs and experiences they have had. However, as your career proceeds and as you have more diverse experiences, a functional resumé can better help you relate your experiences to one another and to tell a coherent story. This exercise will help you convert a chronological resumé into a functional resumé so you will have both versions readily available for use when job hunting at different times in your career.

Instructions

Step 1

The chronological resumé is the starting point for any resumé development, and there are many good resources to help you. You can go to your school's career center, the library, or the Internet to find standard career development books that will provide details on how to format some basic resumé sections. Such sections with standard headings typically include: contact information, objective statement, education, experiences, awards/honors, skills, community activities (e.g., volunteer work), and so forth. If you already have a chronological resumé, make sure your contact information, education, work experiences, and skills listed are all up to date and complete.

Over time with a chronological resumé, you just keep adding your new experiences to become the first entries. However, in a functional resumé, you will have to integrate your experiences in a way that makes sense to the story you want to tell, connects the seemingly unconnected parts of your background, and guides the reader in understanding why you are well suited for a particular job. Recognize that the items you include in this functional resumé therefore are mainly those that support the story you are trying to tell. Not everything you've done may fit in one story, so some items may not appear on this version of your resumé. Also keep in mind that as your career advances it's highly possible that you will want to emphasize some items and not others. As we said in Part I, "it all gets used," but not all at the same time.

Getting started, we recommend you gather your previous exercises, your chronological resumé, and the "Toolkit of a Good Professional Anthropologist" from Part I. In prior exercises, you already articulated what was anthropological about your past experiences. Now you are ready to emphasize how your skills benefit potential employers by clustering relevant sets of skills under carefully chosen headings that move your story along.

Step 2

Identify a common theme or organizing principle for telling your story. One way to do this is to reflect back on your experience to see what the common threads are and assess why you have held and/or may be drawn to the types of work that you have done. In the example provided, a series of jobs working with older adults reveals an ongoing interest in *life history stories* and choosing to work in settings where such storytelling regularly occurs. Table II.12.1 illustrates how early work experiences share aspects of the central theme with later work experiences. Although the job tasks and responsibilities differ, in hindsight, a natural connection was seen across these experiences.

To do this for yourself, take your chronological resumé and your other materials and highlight key experiences and/or words that seem to go together. It may be easier to look at your experiences from the earliest ones to the most recent, rather than going in reverse chronological order. In

Table II.12.1.   Job History Related to Life History Stories

Type of Work Settings	Job Title	Work Experiences
Older Adult Settings		
Brooklyn Public Library Senior Programs	Intern	Designed an oral history project and collected life histories of older people attending senior programs in local library facilities.
"Whisper Minnesota"	Intern	Worked on televised documentary about older women in Minnesota. Compiled life histories of rural and urban older women.
Nursing Home	Activity assistant	Interviewed residents about their lifelong hobbies/interests; designed related activities.
Neighborhood Senior Center	Program coordinator	Responsible for overseeing daily operation of a senior center serving 1,750 clients annually.
University Settings		
Center on Health Research	Project interviewer	Collected data on stress and health using multiple methods; learned about participants' life stories.
Department of Anthropology	Assistant professor	Taught career development classes; guided students through analyzing their educational and work backgrounds to help them develop coherent "stories" of their training and work experiences to date.

other words, you would start from the bottom of your chronological resumé and work your way upward. You could do this exploration with different color highlighters on paper or with the highlighting function in your
word processing application. Consider why you think your experiences go
together. When you find the pattern, you will be able to name your theme.
Then, create a table like the one in this section to help you piece together
the experiences that share common aspects of your theme.

Once you have your theme, you can organize your specific work experiences and skills in relevant clusters. Here you will once again put your experiences from the most recent to the oldest as is typical of a chronological
resumé. For example, to demonstrate how a theme of *life history stories* is articulated throughout a series of work experiences, the work experiences are
organized under headings related to the types of settings where such storytelling occurred. In the example below, the work experiences related to the
theme of *life history stories* are grouped by setting and from the most recent to
the earliest. In your resumé, don't forget to include actual dates of the job du-
ration as well as the position title, organization, and location.

Sample Resumé Entries: Professional Experiences Working with Life History Stories

University Settings:

Department of Anthropology, Wayne State University, Assistant Professor

Taught career development classes; guided students through analyzing their educational and work backgrounds to help them develop coherent "stories" of their training and work experiences to date

Center on Health Research, Case Western Reserve University, Project Interviewer, Cleveland, Ohio

Worked on research team interviewing community residents about stress and health. Data collection involved using questionnaires, telephone interviewing, and learning about participants' life stories.

Older Adult Settings:

Eastside Neighborhood Services, Seniors' Place Coordinator, Minneapolis, Minnesota

Responsible for overseeing daily operation of a senior center serving 1,700 clients annually. Managed budget, supervised staff and volunteers, planned activity program, and wrote newsletter. Created special reminiscence program for seniors to share and write down their memories.

Texas Terrace Convalescent Center, Activity Assistant

Member of eight-person team planning activities for 194 geriatric residents. Interviewed residents about their lifelong hobbies/interests; designed related activity programming. Charted in-care plans of seventy-five residents.

"Whisper Minnesota," Intern, Minneapolis, Minnesota

Intern for a televised documentary about older women in Minnesota. Compiled life histories of rural and urban older women. Participated in editing information into final presentation format.

Brooklyn Public Library, Intern, Brooklyn, New York

Designed an oral history project and collected life histories of older persons who attended senior programs in the Brooklyn Public Library's facilities for the program's ninetieth anniversary celebration.

Step 3

Once you have a draft version of your functional resumé that has a central theme and entries grouped under relevant headings, share your draft with a career counselor, your mentor, an anthropologist or two, and someone from the area in which you are seeking employment. Ask them to comment on what they might change about how information is presented and why they are recommending that change. Ask them to give feedback on the document's organization, how it could make more sense to the reader, and how well it tells the story of your professional development to where you are today and what you have to offer.

Self-Reflection

Write one to two paragraphs reflecting on the experience of doing this exercise. Compare and contrast the feedback you received from anthropologists, career counselors, and others regarding the content, organization, and emphasis of your resumé versions. In what ways were their suggestions similar or different? What insights did you gain from these different assessments? How can you use that knowledge in the future when designing different versions of your resumé for different audiences to effectively present your anthropological skill set for various kinds of job opportunities?

Follow-Up Activities

- Compare your professional introductions and chronological and functional resumés. In each of these versions, look at how you tell your story and what you emphasize. Make sure you can describe your main points succinctly and practice saying aloud how you convey these to a potential employer.
- Consider the cover letter you would draft to accompany your resumé in different situations. Find a job advertisement or use Exercise 10 above as inspiration and create a letter to accompany your functional resumé that introduces you and articulates why you are the best candidate for that job with that company.

- Try making several other kinds of resumé-style documents, such as these:
    1. Develop a *curriculum vitae* (CV) by expanding your resumé. A CV is sometimes called an "academic resumé" and is typically longer and goes into more detail than a resumé. Use the Internet and ask friends, family, colleagues, or professors for good examples of CVs to help you develop your own.
    2. Create a *personal resumé* where you list everything that is important to you in which you devote your time but may or may not be recognized on the professional version of your resumé (e.g., completing a marathon, being a good friend, being a parent, being a caregiver). This activity will give you a chance to honor your important personal as well as professional accomplishments.

Sample Exercise Completed by Andrea, an Undergraduate Student

---

Step 1

As indicated in the instructions, I gathered my materials.

Step 2

Table II.12.2.   Job Training in Supervising and Providing Assistance

Type of Work Settings	Job Title	Work Experiences
Social Service Agencies		
International Institute of Metropolitan Detroit	Student intern	Assisted director in implementing a diversity mentoring program. Interviewed international students for positions teaching within specific cultural/other contexts.
Social service agency	Field supervisor	Placed senior volunteers in homes to assist them and their family members with home care. Monitored activities of the volunteers. Referred clients to community resources.
Social service agency	Program secretary	Provided clerical and interpersonal support to coworkers and senior volunteers. Help to streamline the processing of information for monthly reports and compliance regulations.
Older Adult Setting		
Nursing home	Geriatric support specialist	Provided care for Alzheimer's patients at various stages of the disease. Assisted them with activities of daily living and logged daily progress and issues to report to director and family members.
School Settings		
Business college	Financial aid officer	Counseled students concerning the financing of their education and future career goals. Managed and reconciled the student loan and grant databases.
Public university	Student assistant/ computer lab monitor	Monitored and assisted students in computer applications.

Sample Professional Experiences Working in the Nonprofit Field

Older Adult Settings

Boulevard Temple Nursing Home—Asbury Hall, Geriatric Support Specialist

Cared for high functioning seniors with various stages of Alzheimer's disease in an apartment type setting; assisted them with activities of daily living to help retain abilities.

Social Service Agencies:

Catholic Social Services of Wayne County—Senior Companion Program, Field Supervisor

Trained, placed, and monitored the activities of senior volunteers in homes within the community; managed over fifty volunteers and their file information to be in compliance with federal, state, and local funding sources; and led fund-raising events.

Catholic Social Services of Wayne County—Senior Companion Program, Program Secretary

Instrumental in streamlining office procedures; compiled monthly reports for federal, state, and local funding sources; maintained volunteer and client files with concern for confidentiality; provided desktop publishing for annual program events; assisted the director and staff with in-service trainings.

Higher Education Settings:

Lewis College of Business—Financial Aid Officer

Counseled students about financial aid and educational financing; assisted the director in the administration of all federal, state, and institutional financial aid funds; maintained the college's direct student loan program and all software associated with the financial aid program.

Wayne State University—Computer Lab Monitor/Student Assistant Departments of Anthropology and Political Science

Assisted students with trouble shooting computer problems; monitored and reported computer problems; and addressed issues of concern for students and professors within a particular program.

Andrea's Self-Reflection   I found the resumé exercise a useful rather than stressful task because it helps you to focus on your strengths rather than your weaknesses. By grouping my jobs into categories I was able to visually see my tendency to move toward jobs that involved assisting and counseling a variety of people within different settings. In comparing my chronological resumé with this version, I saw more of myself in it as opposed to a factually oriented "date of work"-based resumé. Using the table initially helped me to be concise and to focus on the skills that I am most proud of in my work history and prepare me to address those things in any future interviews.

EXERCISE 13

Representing Your Body of Work

The Portfolio Exercise

Activity Overview

Creating a portfolio enables you to showcase a broader range of materials than a summary document like a resumé. A portfolio can provide a multidimensional, multimedia format for presenting your interests, skills, and achievements as well as a sense of who you are as a person. Students in disciplines like art or graphic design create portfolios to visually display their work as part of their training. In graphic fields, portfolios are usually visual representations in the form of sketches, artwork, or photos. In anthropology, you may be representing different kinds of work that you have done; for example, you may want to include photos from a fieldsite as well as a more text-heavy document, like a paper you wrote about the fieldwork. This exercise will help you collect, describe, and represent your work to others.

Instructions

Step 1

The first step is to gather materials that will be useful for representing who you are and the work you have done so far. It is recommended that you start by creating one or a series of folders (either hard copy or on your computer). At the outset, put anything in here that you think is a meaningful part of your background; you may end up putting a wide range of professional and personal items here. Such items could include personal information, education history, work experience, awards or other forms of recognition, professional association memberships, coursework projects or assignments completed, presentations, papers, slides, or videos, personal activities, hobbies, or volunteer jobs, goals, plans, or personal values, and so forth.

The metaphor of an expandable file folder is an apt one here—you may look at the various kinds of evidence you have collected and create some broad overarching sections such as academics, work experiences, extracurricular activities, personal, and so forth. You will then subsequently organize your materials within each of these sections. To begin with, each section within your portfolio might be rather basic, and you may make it more intricate over time. A basic version of your academic section might include a list of courses that you took and their descriptions, term papers/projects that you produced, and a statement about what you learned/skills gained. A more elaborate version of your academic section might include writing samples from classes, photos from your field school experience in a foreign country, a report you wrote at the end of the field school for the local community, and a description/photos of you presenting this material at the local school. You might also include a personal reflection on what this experience meant to you and what you learned from it. This personal reflection could be a written document or a slideshow of photos of you in the field accompanied by local music and/or you narrating your account.

By first assembling everything you think you may want to incorporate, you will better be able to assess what fits well together and aids in telling the story of you as an anthropologist. If you want to, you could even make two versions of your portfolio—one which is more personal, like a multi-dimensional diary, which you use for thinking about your own career development over time and reflecting on the meaning of different experiences and pieces of evidence that you are displaying to represent them, and then a more finished product such as a website you use to market yourself and demonstrate your experiences, knowledge, skills, and worldview to potential employers.

Step 2

Create a table like Table II.13.1 or draw a diagram of what will go where in your portfolio to tell the story of you as an anthropologist. Within each of your major sections, think about what subsections could be grouped to show who you are and that would best reflect your accomplishments and relate to your current job searching. In the first column, write down each major section that you wish to build into your portfolio. In the second column, detail the subsections that are part of the larger section. In the third column, list the materials that you want to link to that section. In the fourth column, articulate the skills demonstrated for each section. Make sure that people can clearly understand how the broad sections and information contained within each of them reflect what you have learned and your anthropological skills. (Again, you may want to consult the Toolkit of a Good Professional Anthropologist presented in Part I as well as your prior exercises to figure out how

Table II.13.1.   Sample Basic Portfolio Purpose: To Highlight my Knowledge/Skills in Cultural Anthropology, Overseas Experiences in Latin America, Foreign Language Abilities, Interest in Food and Culture

Section	Subsections	Materials	Skills Demonstrated
Academic work	1. Coursework (highlight coursework in anthropology, area studies, foreign language) 2. Practicum experience: Internship in English as second language teaching agency	1. Final papers from classes 2. Internship project materials developed	1. Anthropological and specific culture area knowledge 2. Writing and analytic capabilities 3. Foreign language skills 4. Project management
Professional experience	1. Instructor—Introduction to Anthropology 2. Spanish tutor 3. Office receptionist	1a. Course syllabus 1b. Statement of teaching philosophy 1c. Reviews of teaching 2. List of skills gained from experience	1. Ability to work independently and with variety of people 2. Positive feedback on teaching style 3. Applicability of skills learned on job 4. Statements from several students I tutored about how I helped them in learning a foreign language

(continued)

Table II.13.1. *(continued)*

Section	Subsections	Materials	Skills Demonstrated
Personal profile	1. Travel experience 2. Volunteer positions held	1. Pictures from trip to Ecuador 2. List of skills developed from volunteer position teaching English in village grade school 3. Picture of me in local classroom setting 4. Pictures of me learning from elder women in village how to cook special regional dishes 5. Post some recipes of regional dishes I learned to cook while living in the village—give credit to those who taught me 6. Post additional recipes I created that are a fusion of what I learned there and how I used these influences on my own cooking style back home 7. Include a video clip of me winning an award for one of these dishes in local cable TV network's cooking contest	1. Applicability of skills learned from volunteer experience 2. Demonstration of love of food and culture 3. Photo, video, and communication skills

to best present your material for each section.) Always keep in mind to portray what your chosen materials demonstrate about you and why these would benefit your potential employer. Finally, consider what is the best scheme for you to tell your own story—should the sections be organized chronologically, thematically, or in some other way?

Step 3

Find a way to display your portfolio. Will you put your portfolio in a book, or a folder, or create your own website? Will you bring it with you to interviews or professional conferences, or will you be able to direct people to a website? Show it to your mentor, a friend, or someone who is not familiar with you or your work and get their feedback. You could do this at a professional conference or at a job fair or even with a professor you've never taken classes from.

Self-Reflection

What did you learn from going through the process of creating your portfolio? How hard or easy was it for you to figure out how to tell the story of yourself as an anthropologist? What do you think about textual representation of your work compared to graphic representation? Which is easier for others to understand and why? Write a short paragraph comparing the value of the written format to the visual format and decide what works best for you and your work. How do you think that your portfolio will continue to grow and change over time?

Follow-Up Activities

- Pretend you are in a job interview situation with a friend or advisor and practice showing your portfolio, describing its contents succinctly, and answering questions.
- Look for examples of portfolios on the Internet. Many students and professionals have online portfolios. Use these for inspiration to make yours even better!

Sample Exercise by Mary, a Ph.D. Student
and Part-time Faculty Member

Step 1

I have known for a long time that I would someday need to organize and construct a teaching portfolio that would highlight my work experience and areas of interest. Knowing I needed to accomplish this task and doing it, however, are two very different things. I am therefore happy to have this opportunity to work through this exercise and share some of my pain with you. The first step is to ask a series of questions: What do I want to showcase in my portfolio? What do I want the finished product to say about me as a student, as a teacher, and as an anthropologist? What should I include and where is it? I began by using categories that would commonly appear on a CV or resumé: personal data, education, teaching experience, and so forth. The next step was to think about how I could expand this information in order to make this product more interesting and more alive. I am a very visual person and a portfolio allows the inclusion of a variety of materials that are not appropriate in a resumé. I can add papers, PowerPoint presentations, and photos describing my work and my travels. I initially focused on developing a teaching portfolio, but while thinking it through I felt a complete picture of my academic life might be more useful. After all, I can always modify my presentation to fit my needs once I have the materials organized and formatted.

Step 2

I constructed a table (Table II.13.2) beginning with organizing categories, including sections, subsections, materials, and skills demonstrated. Column 3 lists the types of materials I would include in each section—although I have not yet selected specific pieces. By grouping my thoughts in chunks like this I am better able to recall and then organize the work I want to highlight. I am finding the Skills Demonstrated column very helpful in making decisions about what to include—what do I want to say about myself? What skills are future employers expecting and how can I best highlight them?

What to include in the portfolio is the first and probably most important question to answer; however, how to display the information and in what order is equally important. I went online and searched out several portfolios—both students and professors—to see how others have presented their material on their websites. I think the order can be flexible and probably dependent on what the purpose of the portfolio is at any given time. I definitely did not like the examples that were presented in chronological order. They were rather tedious to read and it would be harder to explore particular areas of interest to the audience. Then of course there is the underlying question of whether I need to have a website or not.

Table II.13.2. Mary's Basic Portfolio Contents

Section	Subsections	Materials	Skills Demonstrated
Academic	• Degrees • Scholarships • Coursework (list relevant courses with brief descriptions)	• list degrees/dates • list scholarships/dates • papers/projects • PowerPoint Presentations	• academic achievement • academic rewards • demonstrate specific culture areas and scope of knowledge • project management • language skills
Teaching	• Positions held • Classes taught • Curriculum planning	• list GTA dates and part-time faculty assignments • list courses taught with description • examples of syllabi, exams, quizzes, study guides, special projects, PowerPoint presentation • assist in planning of new courses-syllabi • teaching philosophy • teaching evaluations	• proven ability to teach varied courses • ability to plan curriculum and materials • willingness to assist student learning effectiveness
Research	• Projects • Grants • Dissertation	• descriptions • area of study • funding • prospectus	• project design • project management • work independently and in group • technical skills • interview skills • accomplish goals/manage time
Publications	• in progress		• scholarly writings
Travel/Study	• Benin, West Africa • Santiago de Cuba, Cuba • Dias de los Muertos	• slide show of trip—learning and fun • papers • presentations	• fieldwork skills • data management • analysis

Related Business Experience	• Business owner/office manager • Research manager	• public relations firm • business reporting—4 reports yearly	• managerial skills • work independently • research skills • technical skills • people skills
Personal	• Personal data • Professional/student organizations • Volunteer Positions	• American Anthropological Association • Society for the Anthropology of Religion • Anthropology Graduate Student Organization (WSU) • Executive Women International • Harper Woods Homeowners Assn. • Boy Scouts Troop 148 • Cub Scouts Troop 148	• ability to work well with people • plan and organize events • long-term support • leader and committee member

Step 3

After much consideration I have come to the conclusion that it would be most useful to format the information I have gathered for this portfolio in three different ways, each of which would have its specific uses and advantages. The first piece would be a single sheet of paper printed on both sides that would contain a condensed version of my portfolio/CV information (see Tables II.13.3 and II.13.4). This piece would work as an introductory piece I could use to give to new professors or researchers I might be working with or people I meet at conferences. The piece could easily be kept on file and would be a synopsis of my work and achievements along with my personal data.

The second piece would look more like a traditional portfolio—approximately fifty pages with dividers and spiral bound (see Textbox II.13.1). This piece would be printed on my color printer to get the full effect of the color photography and PowerPoint examples that would be included. I would bring this document to interviews as it would contain selected samples of my work.

Table II.13.3.   Mary's Portfolio Display: Side 1: 8½ by 11

Mary Durocher
address
phone
email

Academic Portfolio

Wayne State University

Awards/Scholarships

Graduate Professional Scholarship 2008–2009
Wayne State University
Graduate School

Barbara Aswad Travel Award
Anthropology Department
Wayne State University
2008

Graduate Professional Scholarship 2004–2005
Wayne State University
Graduate School

Office of Global Education,
Wayne State University
Student Study Abroad Grant:
April 2002
Student Study Abroad Grant:
April 2003

Travel

Benin, West Africa, 2002
WSU West Africa Study Trip in with University of Abomey-Calavi, The Beninese Centre for Foreign Language. Focused on African societies in a global manner; with an emphasis on history, politics, social change, religion, literature, and art. Paper: WEST AFRICA STUDY TRIP: Cotonou, Benin, West Africa

Photo by Mary Durocher.

Santiago de Cuba, May 2003
WSU Cuba Study IV with hosted by the Universidad Médico, Faculty #2, Santiago de Cuba. Focused on healthcare, education systems, and religious institutions
Paper: Santería: Finding Parallel Paths

(continued)

Table II.13.3. (*continued*)

Research Projects Worked On

- Wayne State University Research Enhancement Program Grant (171842) English Department

- "Other Worlds": An Ethnographic Study of Personal Accounts of Return of the Dead and Other Mystical Experiences in Health-Related Contexts

- "Interdisciplinary Health Sciences" at Wayne State University (IHS)

- "Being an 'ADHD Teen': Disorder as Lived Experience"

- "Hunters and Gatherers at Wayne State Un versity"

Degrees Granted at Wayne State University
BA—2003
MA—2005
Ph.D. Candidate—2008

Photo by Mary Durocher.

San Antonia, Texas, 2008
Dias de los Muertos—Preliminary fieldwork for dissertation research.

Table II.13.4. Mary's Portfolio Display: Side 2

Coursework

Cultural
Introduction Anthropology
Cultures of the World
Cross Cultural Study of Gender
History of Anthropology
The Ethnography
Studies in Folklore
Latin American Culture
Studying American Culture
Directed Study/Life Stories
Directed Study/End-of-Life Stories
Language and Culture
Language and Societies
Discourse Analysis
War and Culture

Religion
Magic Religion and Science
Anthropology of Religion
Seminar in Religion
Directed Study/Myths

Africa
Cultural Area of Study
Understanding Africa
Cultures of Sub-Saharan Africa

Teaching
Wayne State University
Detroit, Michigan,
Anthropology Department
- Part-time Faculty
  Spring/Summer 2007
  Spring/Summer 2008
- Graduate Teaching Assistantship
  2007–2008
  2006–2007
  2005–2006

ANT 2100
Introduction to Anthropology

ANT 3200
Lost Cities and Ancient Civilizations

ANT 6680/7630
Anthropology of Religion: Myth,
Ritual, and The Gift

Photo by Mary Durocher.

Papers
- *Appliques of the Kings of Dahomey*
- *Legends, Myths and Proverbs in Yoruba-based Divination*
- **Discourse Events and Scrapbook Construction**
- *Umbanda: A New Syncretic Religion in Brazil's Religious Marketplace*
- *Objects of Power as Art in Sub-Saharan Africa Life Stories*
- *A Comparison of Methods in Representing a Sense of Self*

Presentations
Framing Kinship Ties Through Scrapbooking
Central States Anthropological Society,
82nd Annual Meeting
Presented: March 11, 2005

Appliques of the Kings of Dahomey
SOARS, Wayne State University,
Oakland Center
Research conducted in Benin, West
Africa

(*continued*)

Table II.13.4. *(continued)*

- *Cuba*
  Cultural Area of Study

- *Method/Theory*
  Anthropological Methods Anthropology
    Theory I
  Anthropological Theory II
  Qualitative Research I
  Qualitative Research II
  Grantwriting
  Applied Anthropology

- *Spanish*

- *Introduction to Archaeology*
  Lost Cities and Ancient Civilizations
  Material Culture

- *Introduction to Physical Anthropology*
  Biology and Culture
  Introduction to Forensic Science

Teaching Philosophy

I believe that we all learn
something new every day. It is my
responsibility as a teacher to offer
opportunities for learning—to teach
but also to question—to listen and
to provide support for the students'
journeys into anthropology. In my
classes I provide an array of
learning experiences; however as
an anthropologist I focus on
teaching "participant observation"
of the world around us.

Wayne State University Anthropology
    Club
2002 Study Abroad Programs—October
    16, 2002
Students Share Their Cross-Cultural
    Experiences and Research in Africa
    and Cuba
Topic: *A Traveler's Guide to Africa*

Volunteer
- American Anthropological
  Association
- Society for the Anthropology of
  Religion
- Anthropology Graduate Student
  Organization (WSU)
- Executive Women International
- Harper Woods Homeowners Assn.
- Boy Scouts Troop 148

Textbox II.3.1.   Sample Table of Contents for Printed Academic Portfolio

Academic Portfolio
  Mary Durocher
  Address
  Phone
  email

Academic
  Degrees
    BA
    MA—Thesis Abstract—*Framing Kinship Ties Through Scrapbooking*
    Ph.D. Candidate—Thesis Topic—*Exploring Sacred Objects and Their
    Meanings in Catholic Hispanic Households: Domestic Religious
    Practices in Southwest Detroit*
  Scholarships/Grants
  Courses
    List of Relevant Courses & Descriptions
    Research Papers/Presentations
    • *Appliques of the Kings of Dahomey*
    • *Legends, Myths & Proverbs in Yoruba-based Divination*
    • *Discourse Events and Scrapbook Construction*
    • *Umbanda: A New Syncretic Religion in Brazil's Religious Marketplace*
    • *Objects of Power as Art in Sub-Saharan Africa Life Stories*
    • *A Comparison of Methods in Representing a Sense of Self*
    • *Guns and Horses: Changing Military Patterns on the Great Plains*

Teaching
  Part-time Faculty—Spring/Summer 2007, Spring/Summer 2008
  Graduate Teaching Assistantship—2007–2008, 2006–2007, 2005–2006
    • Wayne State University, Detroit, Michigan, Anthropology Department
    • ANT 2100 Introduction to Anthropology
    • ANT 3200 Lost Cities and Ancient Civilizations
    • ANT 6680/7630 Anthropology of Religion: Myth, Ritual, and the Gift
      Course Materials
      Teaching Evaluation
  Teaching Philosophy

(*continued*)

Textbox II.3.1. (*continued*)

Research
Wayne State University Research Enhancement Program Grant (#171842)
Part-time faculty assignment from 7/07 to 8/07 & 7/08-8/08—English
Department
"Other Worlds": An Ethnographic Study of Personal Accounts of Return of
the Dead and Other Mystical Experiences in Health-Related Contexts
"Interdisciplinary Health Sciences" at Wayne State University (IHS)
"Being an 'ADHD Teen': Disorder as Lived Experience"
Dissertation proposal: *Exploring Sacred Objects and Their Meanings in*
Catholic Hispanic Households: Domestic Religious Practices in
Southwest Detroit

Publications

Travel/Study
Benin, West Africa
    Slide Presentation
    Paper: *WEST AFRICA STUDY TRIP: Cotonou, Benin, West Africa*
Santiago de Cuba, Cuba
    Slide Presentation
    Paper: *Santería: Finding Parallel Paths*

Related Business Experience
"MICHIGAN 100" Program (1979–1996) *Business Confidence Index*,
senior officer performance reporting
Michigan Private 100, ranking the state's fastest growing privately held
companies
Michigan Public 100, ranking the state's publicly traded companies
Michigan Growth 100, ranking the publicly traded companies by growth
rate for the previous five years

Personal
American Anthropological Association
    Sections: Central States and Anthropology of Religion
Anthropology Graduate Student Organization (AGSO),
    founding member, current president
Anthropology Club, Wayne State University
Clinton Township Historical Commission, archaeological fieldwork
Executive Women International—former member and secretary
Harper Woods Homeowners Association—founding member and secretary
Detroit Special Olympics—former committee member and volunteer

A more complete portfolio could be established on a website. This is a very exciting idea. I cannot only showcase my work to its best advantage, it also allows me to keep all of my work together in one organized place. I hesitate though in having the website open to the public. I am aware that there are research, legal, and intellectual property issues that I would need to explore further before I take that step. I think a solution would be to keep my website private for now until I do more research on the issues involved. Another solution would be to have the same information on a disc or DVD that I could hand out to interested parties. The website would contain the same categories as the other pieces but allow me to include more samples and many more photographs, sound, video, and PowerPoint presentations.

Mary's Self-Reflection   This exercise was time-consuming but ultimately very useful. I now have the beginnings of several pieces that highlight my academic and teaching accomplishments in different ways. I am particularly happy with the one-page summary. I think I will find many uses for this type of document—perhaps to hand out when joining a new research team, for example. The larger portfolio piece will play a role when applying for teaching positions. That would be the time when someone would be interested in seeing samples of my work particularly copies of syllabi, exams, student assignments, and teacher evaluations. This expanded printed format also works well for including examples of Power-Point presentations and slide shows. I find that much of my work is visually oriented—including the papers. The types of material culture I work with are often unfamiliar to others, and it helps to be able to include photographs with my work. For example, one paper I am quite proud of is titled "Appliques of the Kings of Dahomey." The term "appliques" is not familiar to everyone, and without an idea of what these appliques look like it is very difficult to understand their meanings.

The larger printed portfolio and the website will allow me to take full advantage of the graphic possibilities, for example, I could include the following photos from my field site. I am even now imagining what types of music and video I can add to my portfolio that would better show the various rituals I have observed. More extensive use of sound and video would certainly be something to contemplate in the future. I consider this portfolio-building exercise the first step on a journey that will last throughout my career.

Mary's Fieldwork Photos.

Photo by Mary Durocher.

Photo by Mary Durocher.

EXERCISE 14

Representing Yourself in Other Fields

The Second Domain Exercise

Activity Overview

Now that you have spent a significant amount of time learning how to understand and represent yourself as an anthropologist, you are ready to consider how a related field can benefit from this perspective. This exercise will help you explore another career area—a second domain—that is complemented by an anthropological approach. For example, you may be an anthropology major but want to go to law school. How will you apply your anthropological perspective when working within the legal system? As you learn more about your chosen second domain, you will learn how your anthropology background can be linked to this other career area.

Instructions

Step 1

Identify a second domain career area that you are interested in exploring further. You may choose one from the list in Table II.14.1 or select a different area entirely.

Table II.14.1.   Possible Second Domain Careers

Activisim	Fashion	Museum Studies/Museum Work
Advocacy	Fine Arts	Nonprofit
Agriculture	Food and Culture	Nursing
Animal Behavior	Foreign Language/Translation	Nutrition
Archaeology	Forensics	Performing Arts
Architecture	Genetic Counseling	Policing
Art History	Geography	Politics
Beauty	Gerontology	Product Design
Behavioral Sciences	Healthcare	Property Management
Bereavement	History	Public Health
Biology	Human Resources	Public Policy
Botany	Immigration Issues	Publishing
Business	Information Technology	Real Estate
Career Counseling	International Relations	Retail
Child Development	Journalism	Psychology
Creative Writing	Labor Relations	Science
Criminal Justice	Law	Social Work
Design	Library and Information Science	Sports and Leisure
Development	Linguistics	Technology
Education	Marketing	Therapies
Engineering	Manufacturing	Tourism
Environmental Studies	Media	Urban Planning
Epidemiology	Medicine	Urban Studies
Ethics	Military	Women's Studies

Step 2

Research and write a one-page summary description of this career area. In this summary include a brief definition of the field and the kinds of education and professional training needed to work in this field. Discuss the kinds of job opportunities in this area, who works in this field, where most of the jobs in this field are, the pay scale, and why this field is or isn't growing. Report on how you researched this career area. For example, discuss how you learned this information, what information resources were used, websites visited, books or articles read, professional associations or individuals contacted, and so forth.

Step 3

Based on the knowledge you gained about this second domain career area, write a paragraph on how you could combine an anthropological approach with this second domain area. What role can anthropologists play in research, practice, and/or policy formulation relating to this area? To what extent have anthropologists been active in this area? What are some future roles that you could see anthropologists having in this area? If there were barriers to collaboration between anthropologists and others in this area, how could they be overcome? How will you integrate your anthropological background and skill set in this area?

Self-Reflection

Write one or more paragraphs describing in what ways your interest in bringing your anthropological background and skill set to this second domain was heightened or lessened and why. How will this change, if any, affect your choice of second domain? What about in your future?

Follow-Up Activities

- If you did not already have a chance to interview someone who works in the second domain area, set up an informational interview with someone in that field. This could be done face to face if you have the opportunity to set an appointment, over the phone, or over email if your contact is willing to take the time to type out answers to questions. Create a list of questions to ask during your interview time that will give you a deeper understanding of this second domain. Ask about how they came to their current position, what kind of educational training they needed, career trends in that field, advice for someone entering the field, and so forth.
- If you already did your first interview described above, plan another interview with someone else. Concisely give an account of what you learned about the second domain area. Ask them if the impressions you have formed of this area are accurate and correspond with their views of this field. Ask them to correct, clarify, and further elaborate on what you would need to know to work in this area. Ask them if they have already or are interested in working with anthropologists. Why or why not? How do they see such multidisciplinary collaborations? What advice would they give you based on your interests and going forward in your education? For example, do they think you should consider undertaking certain specific types of training, take certain courses, or do particular types of internships?

Sample Exercise Completed by Monica, a Ph.D. Student

Step 1

Before discussing my second domain, I think it is first important to say what my first domain is. I am interested in applied medical anthropology. I have become extremely interested in anthropological methods and training while trying to find a way to incorporate that with the community, so I would like to be involved in projects within and outside academia.

My second domain area is public health research. By *research* I mean working at a research company or group that primarily conducts research. I have worked for two research companies over the past six years and I am familiar with the very specific ways these companies conduct their projects.

Step 2

The second domain area I chose to pursue for this project is public health research. Initially, I pursued this area with the intent of learning how different research companies incorporate interdisciplinary researchers. I was also interested in learning more about a university-based research organization in order to compare what I had learned to what I already know about the private nonprofit research organization I had worked for.

I approached this exercise by asking myself what I would be doing at this moment if I was not actively working in any area of anthropology. This became a difficult question at first because applied anthropologists often work under titles that do not use the word "anthropologist" to describe an area of work that incorporates everything we are taught in anthropology. My search for a second domain began in the area of public health. I have a master's degree in anthropology and experience working in health-related research and prevention. Combined, my education and employment qualify me for a variety of different areas. I chose research within public health simply because I enjoy researching things, talking to people, and I have always been interested in topics related to health. These were but a few of the perceptions I had before researching this project.

Since I have taken a number of health science classes, I already knew the basics of the public health field, particularly that it is both a "science" and an "art." I was taught that public health is a "science" because it ensures that data are collected systematically and statistics are an important part of research and prevention, but it is also an "art" because you are dealing with people. Although the numbers are extremely informative, the humanistic side is necessary to effectively understand why people do what they do and how health programs can be effectively implemented. Public health is also interdisciplinary. Although applied anthropology can involve the application of anthropology outside the traditional areas of the discipline, public health incorporates into its very definition the use of a diverse array of fields that are not traditionally associated with medicine.

Medicine and public health at first seem to be synonymous but are actually quite different in scope. Medicine deals with an individual disease in an individual person that the doctor treats. Public health might also look at a disease but will see how that disease affects the population looking at the overall picture. In order to find out what the overall picture is, public health uses an interdisciplinary approach incorporating disciplines ranging from anthropology to engineering. As a result, the jobs available in public health and the requirements for them are extremely diverse. Research jobs at the master's degree level require that you have some experience and interest in the health of populations, along with some type of background in statistics. In order to learn about the jobs available in public health, I first looked at a Pfizer 2002 publication (DeBuono and Tilson 2002) that describes numerous jobs in public health. To name a few, the jobs described ranged from state epidemiologist, behavioral science, journalist, to lawyer. The title "researcher" is never independently mentioned but is incorporated into many of the job descriptions in the book. For example, there are several jobs like "research epidemiologist" and "mental health researcher" that formally incorporate "researcher" into the title. Other jobs use "researcher" as part of the description in the text. In the "profiling the job" section under "family health nutritionist" DeBuono and Tilson (2002) state that "universities and private laboratories have an ongoing need for nutritionists as researchers and professors" (p. 65). Researchers are basically in every part of public health and are needed for a wide range of projects.

In order to find public health research jobs that I could qualify for I did an online search of "Public Health Career Mart" with little success. Even though I was able to find several jobs that I qualified for, the vast majority required a Ph.D. or a Dr.P.H. I had more success searching the "monster" website, but I also viewed individual companies that I was familiar with like RAND and the Los Angeles Department of Health Services (LADHS) where I had further success. Most of these jobs seemed to be midlevel, manager-type positions overseeing other employees while working under a more senior researcher. It seemed that regardless of their specific requirements they all "preferred" the master's degree and required some background in statistics as well as some experience in the field. The specific major did not appear to be essential as long as these other requirements were met but could serve positively depending on what they were looking for.

Since the public health research positions I qualify for appear to be midlevel, it seems that there are many positions available across the country particularly in large metropolitan areas. Many of these positions were for research companies, universities (or university projects), and health insurance companies for the most part. It appeared that there were plenty of jobs if the applicant is flexible about the location, which I would be. The salary was not always discussed and few job announcements specifically mentioned it. LADHS listed a job for a research analyst as ranging from $3,362–$3,948 per month but most stated that it depended on experience. A lot of these jobs were listed for MA level candidates, but people with more experience or academic degrees were also qualified to apply. Many of these positions are graded, so I would imagine that a person may want to come into one of these positions in order to gain experience and work their way up to other positions within the same company so these types of jobs may still be an option for me with the Ph.D. Overall, it appeared that there were a great number of jobs in this area and that public health is another place where I can look for jobs after graduation.

Step 3

Anthropology can be easily combined with public health. Anthropology contributes a skill set that other health professionals and social scientists do not have but is essential in gaining a deeper understanding of the science and art of public health. This exercise taught me that I can apply my skills as an anthropologist to public health, but I have to understand what is important to public health. One of those things important to public health is statistics. Even though public health research is often conducted using the expertise of specialists working in teams, the "language" spoken and understood by the majority of these professionals is numbers, so it is important to have at the very least a basic understanding of what that means in public health. Many studies use survey research and methods using scales. If you are going to be working in public health these are things that may be standard in the research. Even though the anthropologist may not be directly involved in that aspect of the work, it is important to have a solid understanding of that aspect in order to be able to explain the "numberless" qualitative work (that many of them will not be familiar with and may dismiss as "unscientific" because of their lack of experience and understanding of it).

Monica's Self-Reflection The second domain I chose to research for this project was public health research. When I started this project I knew a little about it because I had taken course work in health science and had worked in research and promotion, but I had never taken a great deal of time to look at the jobs that were available in the area. Additionally, even though I knew public health was interdisciplinary and many anthropologists work directly in public health, my experiences with them had been separate. The anthropologists I knew working in research were in high-level positions and they had been hired specifically for their skills as anthropologists. They had many years of experience following their Ph.D.s prior to working at that organization. As a person with only a master's degree, I was not completely aware of the types of positions that were available for someone at this level outside the field of anthropology. This project allowed me to see the type of positions that are available to me now and how I can incorporate them into my life in the future. It also showed me that our training in anthropology provides us with a unique set of skills that is completely compatible with other disciplines like public health.

I was extremely interested in my second domain area before I did this exercise. If I had decided not to continue with my studies in anthropology, public health is the area where I would have searched for employment. One thing that I learned in this job search is that many of the positions are graded, meaning that you are hired at a certain level and can work your way up in the company. Even though many of the positions prefer a master's degree, many of these positions are also good starting points either to work in immediately after getting your degree or before if possible. Many of these sites also had more advanced entry-level positions that I can consider when I near or when I actually graduate. It appeared that most wanted a person who could use the skills he or she had learned rather than a person in a very specific area of study. Someone I spoke to in the field seemed to corroborate this since she has been working in public health research for over twenty years and does not have any type of degree in public health.

Monica's References

DeBuono, B. A., and H. Tilson. (2002). *Advancing Healthy Populations: The Pfizer Guide to Careers in Public Health*. Retrieved from www.pfizercareerguides.com/. New York: Pfizer Inc.

McKenzie, J. F., R. Pinger, and J. Kotecki. (1999). *An Introduction to Community Health*, 3rd ed. Boston: Jones and Bartlett Publishers.

Monica's Websites

Association of Schools of Public Health
www.asph.org

Los Angeles Department of Health Services
http://easier.co.la.ca.us/jobs/cfscripts/search_body.cfm

Monster
www.monster.com

Public Health Career Mart
www.apha.org/career

RAND Corporation
www.rand.org/jobs/

What Is Public Health? web page
www.whatispublichealth.org

EXERCISE 15

Representing Your Whole Anthropological Career

The Retirement Speech Exercise

Activity Overview

This exercise is designed to help you take a long-term perspective on your career. You will imagine that you are giving a speech at your own retirement party. Although it may seem a long way off to envision yourself retiring, it is very useful to consider what work you really want to do over time and what would be meaningful to you. Imagine where you will end up in your career. In a retirement speech, you would also typically thank people who helped you and provided mentorship along the way. This exercise gives you a chance to think more deeply about these issues, build on what you have learned by doing earlier exercises in the book, and create a guiding document that you can return to and modify as your career progresses over time.

Instructions

Step 1

Write a fictive retirement speech for yourself. You can either make up your own format or use the template provided in Table II.15.1 to help you with getting started and organizing your ideas. Fill in the relevant names and skills that you imagine will be true when you reflect back on your career.

Table II.15.1. Retirement Speech Template

Thank you for coming to my retirement party today. It means a lot to me to see all of these people whom I have known and worked with for such a long time. On this occasion, I would like to say a few words about what working in _____ field has been like for me. When I was graduating from college and thinking about entering this field, I thought the work would be _____ and involve _____ . But there were a few surprises along the way like _____ that I did not expect but were very important for _____ reasons.

As an anthropologist, I originally expected to use _____ , and _____ skills from my education and background in doing this work. In reality, this work called for _____, _____ , and _____. I learned these additional skills by doing _____ , and knowing them has enabled me to _____ .

At this point, there are some people that I would like to thank who helped me over the course of my career. [List people here and what you would like to thank them for. You may want to include family, teachers, real or fictive bosses, and mentors. Don't just list them by name but say what each has done for you. Feel free to also imagine people whom you believe may be important for your career in the future.]

To wrap up, when I began my career, I did not envision that would occur and that it would lead to _____ . When that happened, I felt _____ . This work has been highly meaningful for me due to _____ . Someone recently asked me what I would like my legacy to be and how I would like others to think about my career and contributions. What I said to this person was _____ . The advice I would give to someone starting out and entering this type of career is _____ . In closing, I would like to say _____ . Again, thank you all very much for coming today.

Self-Reflection

Write one or two paragraphs reflecting on the experience of creating this retirement speech. You may discuss why this activity was easy or difficult for you to do and what you learned from doing it, such as what you discovered about how you view your work life, your anthropological skill set, important people in your life, and so forth. Think about how you can use this information now to work on building your career and taking steps to achieve these goals.

Follow-Up Activities

- Now, make this happen!
- Have a great and fulfilling anthropological career!

> ### *Sample Exercise Completed by Dianna, an MA Student*

Step 1

Thank you for coming to my retirement party tonight. It means a lot to me to see all of these people whom I have known and worked with for such a long time. On this occasion, I would like to say a few words about what working in archaeology specifically and anthropology generally has meant to me. When I was graduating from college and thinking about entering this field, I thought that working in an academic research environment would be intellectually challenging and that I would make great contributions in archaeology and anthropology. But there were a couple of surprises along the way. For example, the most important person on an archaeological project can be the cook! I naively thought it would be me, and I did not expect my role as a researcher to take a back seat to a good meal at the end of the day in the field. However, it was an important revelation as I soon realized that being an archaeologist involves more than learning about the past, but also keeping the living (the crew) content. As an archaeologist, I originally expected to mainly apply the methods and theory I learned during my college education in the working world as well as any hands-on experience I was able to absorb along the way. In reality leading archaeological teams in conducting research called for skills in counseling, relationships, communication, negotiating, and playing the role of arbitrator. I learned these additional skills by first fulfilling the role of assistant to a director that perfected (impressively I might add) the fine art of pleasing the crew. Learning by imitation and putting these skills into practice enabled me to be involved in and then lead many worthwhile and interesting archaeological projects over the years.

At this point, there are some people I would like to thank who helped me over the course of my career. First and foremost without the support of my immediate family during my "career" as a full-time student, I would not be standing here today as an archaeologist. Their emotional and financial support was crucial for my success. They have always been proud and genuinely happy for me and all of my successful endeavors. Academically, there are two special people that stand out in my mind and supported me while I was a student and have been with me in spirit after I left armed with my degree as I entered the "real" world. My main professor was at first an enigma, then an advisor, a mentor, and finally a friend. Never did his support waver; nor did he think any goal was too high for me to reach. He inspired me to work diligently and I owe him a debt of gratitude for my career. He taught me how to write like an archaeologist, which often meant abandoning my love for creative writing and simply "writing the facts." (Some of you might think that would be the easier task, but believe me, it was *not* the easiest of tasks.) He still encourages, inspires, and has not lost his sense of humor! Another professor was the ultimate cheerleader for students, and I was lucky to be under her positive guidance. Under her tutelage, she encouraged me and always accentuated my talents and focused on my strong attributes. This gave me the confidence I was lacking, and I am eternally grateful. My manager at my first job at an archaeology lab also was influential in my career. He taught me different ways to approach archaeology with an open mind, and I learned technical skills that led me to other projects along the way. Finally, reentering the academic field as a Ph.D. student was a challenge that I met with confidence because of my earlier academic experiences. Many successful archaeologists come from university, and I am proud to count myself as a graduate.

To wrap up, when I began my career, I did not envision that working as a research assistant in the local anthropology museum at the university would open doors to a research career in which I was able to make valuable published contributions in the field of archaeology. It turned out that I could be important—maybe even as important as the cook on the team! When I look back upon these accomplishments, I am humbled to be in the presence of my family, teachers, and friends tonight. Someone recently asked me what I would like my legacy to be and how I would like others to think about my career and contributions. What I said to this person was that I hoped people remembered me for doing great things in archaeology, but more importantly, I hoped they would remember me as a person who had a passion for her work, was fair to work with, taught students well, created a positive learning environment, and made others feel good about themselves. This is how I remember the people in my life that I admire, have learned from, and continue to learn from even today. The advice I would give someone starting out and entering the field of archaeology is stay true to yourself and never think you've learned everything, because that is the precise moment when you stop learning and that would be a disservice to the field and yourself. In closing, I would like to say: I'll always keep digging! Again, thank you for celebrating with me tonight. I've enjoyed every step along the way because it was enriched by all of you.

Dianna's Self-Reflection   This was a great learning experience and a creative way to access career goals. By writing about my future, I was able to more clearly define in my mind some of my ultimate goals. Before writing this speech, my goals were not focused; I felt I would just move along with the wind. I surprised myself in parts and realize now that I really want to conduct research and continue my education. I also realized how difficult it has been this year with an impending graduation. Moving on is twofold; it is exciting to think of the endless possibilities and sad to leave mentors and my advisor behind. I shall miss them more than anything, yet I am proud they prepared me for a successful career in anthropology and archaeology. I think I will keep a copy of this and read it from time to time to put perspective on my goals.

References

Baba, Marietta L. 1986. Business and Industrial Anthropology: An Overview. *NAPA Bulletin* 2.

DeBuono, B. A., and H. Tilson. 2002. *Advancing Healthy Populations: The Pfizer Guide to Careers in Public Health.* New York: Pfizer Inc. Available at www.pfizer careerguides.com.

Ervin, Alexander M. 2004. *Applied Anthropology: Tools and Perspectives for Contemporary Practice.* 2nd ed. Boston: Allyn and Bacon Publishers.

Ferraro, Gary. 2008. *Cultural Anthropology: An Applied Perspective.* 7th ed. Belmont, CA: Wadsworth Publishing.

Fortes , Meyer. 1971. "Introduction." In *The Developmental Cycle of Domestic Groups,* ed. J. Goody (pp. 1–14). Cambridge: Cambridge University Press.

Fry, Christine L. 2003. "The Life Course as a Cultural Construct." In *Invitation to the Life Course,* ed. Richard A. Settersten (pp. 269–294). Amityville, NY: Baywood Publishing Company.

Garcia Ruiz, Carmen. 2000. Toolkit for Professional Anthropologists. *Anthropology News* 41 (3): 44–45.

Gamst, Frederick C. 1995. "Considerations of Work." In *Meanings of Work: Considerations for the Twenty-First Century,* ed. Frederick C. Gamst (pp. 1–45). Albany: State University of New York Press.

Gwynne, Margaret A. 2003. *Applied Anthropology: A Career Oriented Approach.* Boston: Allyn and Bacon Publishers.

Hill, Carole E. 2000. "Strategic Issues for Rebuilding a Theory and Practice Synthesis." In *The Unity of Theory and Practice in Anthropology: Rebuilding A Fractured Synthesis,* eds. Carole E. Hill and Marietta L. Baba. *NAPA Bulletin* 18.

Jordan, Ann T. 2003. *Business Anthropology.* Prospect Heights, IL: Waveland Press.

Kedia, Satish, and John van Willigen, eds. 2005. *Applied Anthropology: Domains of Application.* Westport, CT: Greenwood Publishing Group.

Lamphere, Louise. 2004. The Convergence of Applied, Practicing, and Public Anthropology in the 21st Century. *Human Organization* 63 (4): 431–443.

McKenzie, J. F., R. Pinger, and J. Kotecki. 1999. *An Introduction to Community Health*, 3rd ed. Boston: Jones and Bartlett Publishers.

Mortimer, Jeylan T., and Shanahan, Michael J., eds. 2006. *Handbook of the Lifecourse*. New York: Springer Publishing Company.

National Association of Practicing Anthropologists and American Anthropological Association. 2000. The Toolkit of a Good Professional Anthropologist. *Anthropology News* 41 (3): 44.

Nolan, Riall W. 2003. *Anthropology in Practice: Building a Career Outside of the Academy*. Boulder, CO: Rienner Publishers.

Omohundro, John T. 2001. *Careers in Anthropology*. 2nd ed. Mountain View, CA: Mayfield Publishing Company.

Omohundro, John T. 2007. *Thinking Like an Anthropologist: A Practical Introduction to Cultural Anthropology*. Boston: McGraw-Hill.

Price, Laurie J. 2001. The Mismatch between Anthropology Graduate Training and the Work Lives of Graduates. *Practicing Anthropology* 23 (1): 55–57.

Settersten, Richard A., ed. 2003. *Invitation to the Life Course: Towards New Understandings of Later Life*. Amityville, NY: Baywood Publishing Company.

Simonelli, Jeanne. 2001. Mainstreaming the Applied Track: Connections, Guises, and Concerns. *Practicing Anthropology* 23 (1): 48–49.

Tannen, Deborah. 1994. Who Gets Heard? Talking at Meetings. In *Talking from 9–5*. New York: Aron Books.

Turner, Victor. 1969. *The Ritual Process*. Chicago: Aldine.

Van Gennep, Arnold. 1960. *The Rites of Passage*. MB Vizedom and ST Kimall, trans. Chicago: University of Chicago Press.

van Willigen, John. 2002. *Applied Anthropology: An Introduction*. 3rd ed. Westport, CT: Greenwood Publishing Group.

About the Authors

Sherylyn H. Briller is an assistant professor in the Department of Anthropology and a faculty associate in the Institute of Gerontology and the Center to Advance Palliative Care Excellence at Wayne State University in Detroit, Michigan. She received a Ph.D. in anthropology from Case Western Reserve University. A medical anthropologist who specializes in aging and end-of-life issues, Dr. Briller has a long-standing interest in cross-cultural gerontology and has conducted research in Mongolia and in the United States. Her research program focuses on old-age support mechanisms, long-term care, creating supportive health care settings and end-of-life issues. She coauthored the four-volume series *Creating Successful Dementia Care Settings* (2002) and coedited the volume *End-of-Life Stories: Crossing Disciplinary Boundaries* (2005). As an applied anthropologist, Dr. Briller has published, consulted, and spoken to numerous audiences including academics, policymakers, health care staff, and consumers about health care generally and palliative care specifically. She is a fellow of the Society for Applied Anthropology and president-elect of the Association for Anthropology and Gerontology Education. Dr. Briller is highly interested in the career development of anthropologists and the role of anthropological education in the formation of professional identities. These ongoing interests led to the development of this book.

Amy Goldmacher is a Ph.D. candidate in the Department of Anthropology at Wayne State University in Detroit, Michigan. She received an M.A. in anthropology from Wayne State and a B.A. in anthropology with honors from Grinnell College in Iowa. Prior to graduate school, she spent six years in the publishing industry working in the editorial, marketing, and sales divisions of a college textbook publisher. Currently, she is a graduate teaching assistant in the Department of Anthropology at Wayne State. In addition to conducting research on how anthropology students receive the kind of training that will enable them to find jobs in industry after graduation, she is interested in the relationship of technology and culture and diffusion of innovations.